Learn to Program

Second Edition

Chris Pine

The Pragmatic Bookshelf

Dallas, Texas • Raleigh, North Carolina

Many of the designations used by manufacturers and sellers to distinguish their products are claimed as trademarks. Where those designations appear in this book, and The Pragmatic Programmers, LLC was aware of a trademark claim, the designations have been printed in initial capital letters or in all capitals. The Pragmatic Starter Kit, The Pragmatic Programmer, Pragmatic Programming, Pragmatic Bookshelf, PragProg and the linking *g* device are trademarks of The Pragmatic Programmers, LLC.

Every precaution was taken in the preparation of this book. However, the publisher assumes no responsibility for errors or omissions, or for damages that may result from the use of information (including program listings) contained herein.

Our Pragmatic courses, workshops, and other products can help you and your team create better software and have more fun. For more information, as well as the latest Pragmatic titles, please visit us at *http://pragprog.com*.

Printed in the United States of America.
ISBN-13: 978-1-934356-36-4
Printed on acid-free paper.
Book version: P3.0—October 2011

Contents

Preface to the Second Edition

I ran into an old friend the other day. It's been more than a decade since last we spoke. As we were catching up, I mentioned, "Oh, and I sort of accidentally wrote a book a few years back."

After all, I didn't really *mean* to write this book. Once upon a time, some of us Ruby fans were chatting about teaching programming, and I had a few things to say about it. Not much. Just a few things.

Somehow the conversation migrated onto a wiki somewhere, and I wrote up a few of my ideas. After a while, it seemed like I was the only one writing, so I moved some of my thoughts to my own website. Suddenly I realized it was starting to look suspiciously like a tutorial.

And not a very good one, I have to say.

Well, my initial attempts seemed pretty good to *me*, and I got positive feedback from the other Ruby programmers who saw it. But then again, we all knew how to program. When I actually showed the tutorial to a nonprogrammer (my extremely patient wife), it was clear that there was still much work to be done.

So, I reworked it and rewrote some sections, and it became…better. Not great, though. It took several more iterations before it was really usable. But by then I was hooked: I was going to make this tutorial the best programming tutorial ever! Fortunately, it got plenty of use, I got plenty of feedback, and it continued to improve. (I could never have done it on my own. If it weren't for all the comments and questions, this whole thing never would have gone anywhere.)

And so it went, for about three years. Conversation moves to wiki. Wiki migrates to tutorial. Tutorial becomes book. And at every step, I'm answering as many emails as I can, noting where people are having the most trouble, learning *why* they are having trouble, and smoothing the way for the next programmers-to-be. At every step, it's getting just a tiny bit better.

As it turns out, 5,000 tiny bits really add up.

And now that it's done, I'm convinced I learned more from this book than anyone else did—not about how to program, of course, but about the way we learn programming and about learning in general.

Perhaps the most important principle in teaching programming is to separate concepts as much as possible so that the programmer-to-be has to learn only one concept at a time. This is much easier said than done, though. There were just so many things that I was used to, so I often didn't realize when I was introducing a new concept. With some practice, though, and much help from aspiring programmers, it became easier as I went along.

Naturally, I tried to cover more basic concepts before working up to more complex concepts. I was amazed, however, at how little of a precedence hierarchy there really is. Many of the ideas could be taught meaningfully independently of the others. Eventually, I just had to pick an order, and I tried to arrange things so that each new section was motivated by the previous one.

Another principle I realized early on is the importance of teaching only one way to do something. It's an obvious benefit in a book for people who have never programmed before. For one thing, one way to do something is easier to learn than two. Perhaps the more important benefit, though, is that the fewer things you teach a new programmer, the more creative and clever they have to be with the primitive bits they do know. Since so much of programming is creative problem solving, it's crucial to encourage this as soon as possible.

I tried to piggyback programming concepts onto concepts the new programmer already has and to present ideas in such a way that their intuition will carry the load, rather than the tutorial. Object-oriented (OO) programming lends itself to this quite well. I was able to begin referring to "objects" and different "kinds of objects" pretty early in the tutorial, slipping those phrases in at the most innocent of moments. I wasn't saying anything like "everything in Ruby is an object" or "numbers and strings are kinds of objects," because, beloved as they are in the Ruby community, these statements really don't mean *anything* to a new programmer. Instead, I would talk about strings (not "string objects"), and sometimes I would refer to "objects," simply meaning "the things in these programs." The fact that all these things in Ruby *are* objects (in the OO sense) made this sort of sneakiness on my part work so well.

Although I wanted to avoid needless OO jargon, I did try to make sure that if you do need to learn a word, you learn the right one. (You don't want to have to learn it twice, right?) So, I called them "strings," not "text." Methods needed to be called something, so I just called them "methods."

As far as the exercises are concerned, I think I came up with some good ones, but you can never have too many. Examples were much easier: just come up with some joke that you can relate to the concept you're explaining, and there you go! But exercises...they were hard. Honestly, I bet I spent half of my time just trying to come up with fun, interesting exercises. Almost everything I came up with was just boring, and boring exercises absolutely kill any desire to program. On the other hand, the perfect exercise creates an itch you can't help but scratch. I did my best, but I don't think any of them are perfect. I hope you will come up with your own programming tasks or even just variations on those given here.

I remember someone telling me that they had added a bunch of code to their orange tree program so that it would actually draw an ASCII-art orange tree! It grew as the tree got older and even displayed the correct number of oranges! That's amazingly cool!

A lot of software grows in this way: small, simple beginnings, with tiny improvements here or an interface overhaul there, until you have something much larger than what you started with. I guess books can grow this way, too.

Chris Pine
Oslo, Norway, January 2009

Introduction

I vividly remember writing my first program. (My memory is pretty horrible; I don't vividly remember many things, just things like waking up after oral surgery or watching the birth of our children or that time I was trying to flirt with this girl and she told me that my zipper was down or when I set my shoes on fire in my middle-school gym class or writing my first program...you know, things like that.)

I suppose, looking back, that it was a fairly ambitious program for a newbie (twenty or thirty lines of code, I think). But I was a math major, after all, and we are supposed to be good at things like "logical thinking." So, I went down to the Reed College computer lab, armed only with a book on programming and my ego, sat down at one of the Unix terminals there, and started programming. Well, maybe "started" isn't the right word. Or "programming." I mostly just sat there, feeling hopelessly stupid. Then ashamed. Then angry. Then just small. Eight grueling hours later, the program was finished. It worked, but I didn't much care at that point. It was not a triumphant moment.

It has been more than a decade, but I can still feel the stress and humiliation in my stomach when I think about it.

Clearly, this was *not* the way to learn programming.

Why was it so hard? I mean, there I was, this reasonably bright guy with some fairly rigorous mathematical training—you'd think I would be able to get this! And I did go on to make a living programming, and even to write a book about it, so it's not like I just "didn't have what it took" or anything like that. No, in fact, I find programming to be pretty easy these days, for the most part.

So, why was it so hard to tell a computer to do something only mildly complex? Well, it wasn't the "mildly complex" part that was giving me problems; it was the "tell a computer" part.

In any communication with humans, you can leave out all sorts of steps or concepts and let them fill in the gaps. In fact, you have to do this! We'd never be able to get anything done otherwise. The typical example is making a peanut butter and jelly sandwich. Normally, if you wanted someone to make you a peanut butter and jelly sandwich, you might simply say, "Hey, could you make me a peanut butter and jelly sandwich?" But if you were talking to someone who had never done it before, you would have to tell them how:

1. Get out two slices of bread (and put the rest back).
2. Get out the peanut butter, the jelly, and a butter knife.
3. Spread the peanut butter on one slice of bread and the jelly on the other one.
4. Put the peanut butter and jelly away, and take care of the knife.
5. Put the slices together, put the sandwich on a plate, and bring it to me. Thanks!

I imagine those would be sufficient instructions for a small child. Small children are needlessly, recklessly clever, though. What would you have to say to a computer? Well, let's just look at that first step:

1.
   a. Locate bread.
   b. Pick up bread.
   c. Move to empty counter.
   d. Set down bread on counter.
   e. Open bag of bread.

   ...

But no, this isn't nearly good enough. For starters, how does it "locate bread"? We'll have to set up some sort of database associating items with locations. The database will also need locations for peanut butter, jelly, knife, sink, plate, counter....

Oh, and what if the bread is in a bread box? You'll need to open it first. Or in a cabinet? Or in your fridge? Perhaps behind something else? Or what if it is *already on the counter*? You didn't think of that one, did you? So, now we have this:

- Initialize item-to-location database.
- If bread is in bread box:
  - Open bread box.
  - Pick up bread.
  - Remove hands from bread box.
  - Close bread box.

- If bread is in cabinet:
  - Open cabinet door.
  - Pick up bread.
  - Remove hands from cabinet.
  - Close cabinet door.

...

And on and on it goes. What if no clean knife is available? What if there is no empty counter space at the moment? And you'd better pray to whatever forces you find comfort in that there's no twist-tie on that bread!

Even steps such as "open bread box" need to be explained...and this is why we don't have robots making sandwiches for us yet. It's not that we can't build the robots; it's that we can't program them to make sandwiches. It's because making sandwiches is *hard* to describe (but easy to do for smart creatures like us humans), and computers are good only for things that are (relatively) *easy* to describe (but hard to do for slow creatures like us humans).

And that is why I had such a hard time writing that first program. Computers are way dumber than I was prepared for.

2.1 What Is Programming?

When you teach someone how to make a sandwich, your job is made much easier because they already know what a sandwich is. It is this common, informal understanding of "sandwichness" that allows them to fill in the gaps in your explanation. Step 3 says to spread the peanut butter on one slice of bread. It doesn't say to spread it on only one side of the bread or to use the knife to do the spreading (as opposed to, say, your forehead). You assume they just know these things.

Similarly, I think it will help to talk a bit about what programming is in order to give you a sort of informal understanding of it.

Programming is telling your computer how to do something. Large tasks must be broken up into smaller tasks, which must be broken up into still smaller tasks, down until you get to the most basic tasks that you don't have to describe—the tasks your computer already knows how to do. (These are *really* basic things such as arithmetic or displaying some text on your screen.)

My biggest problem when I was learning to program was that I was trying to learn it backwards. I knew what I wanted the computer to do and tried working backward from that, breaking it down until I got to something the computer knew how to do. Bad idea. I didn't really know what the computer *could* do, so I didn't know what to break the problem down to. (Mind you, now that I do know, this is exactly how I program these days. But it just doesn't work to start out this way.)

That's why you're going to learn it differently. You'll learn first about those basic things your computer can do (a few of them) and then find some simple tasks that can be broken down into a few of these basic things. *Your* first program will be so easy that it won't even take you a minute.

2.2 Programming Languages

To tell your computer how to do something, you must use a programming language. A programming language is similar to a human language in that it's made up of basic elements (such as nouns and verbs) and ways to combine those elements to create meaning (sentences, paragraphs, and novels). There are many languages to choose from (C, Java, Ruby, Perl...), and some have a larger set of those basic elements than others. Ruby has a fine set and is one of the easiest to learn (as well as being elegant and forgiving and the name of my daughter, and so forth), so we'll use that one.

Perhaps the best reason for using Ruby is that Ruby programs tend to be short. For example, here's a small program in Java:

```java
public class HelloWorld {
  public static void main(String []args) {
    System.out.println("Hello World");
  }
}
```

And here's the same program in Ruby:

```ruby
puts 'Hello World'
```

This program, as you might guess from the Ruby version, just writes Hello World to your screen. It's not nearly as obvious from looking at the Java version.

How about this comparison: I'll write a program to do *nothing!* Nothing at all! In Ruby, you don't need to *write* anything at all; a completely blank program will work just fine.

In Java, though, you need all this:

```java
public class DoNothing {
  public static void main(String[] args) {
  }
}
```

You need all that just to do nothing, just to say, "Hey, I am a Java program, and I don't do anything!" So, that's why we'll use Ruby. (My first program was *not* in Ruby, which is another reason why it was so painful.)

2.3 The Art of Programming

An important part of programming is, of course, making a program that does what it's supposed to do. In other words, it should have no bugs. You know all this. However, focusing on correctness, on bug-free programs, misses a lot of what programming is all about. Programming is not just about the end product; it's about the process that gets you there. (Anyway, an ugly process will result in buggy code. This happens every time.)

Programs aren't just built in one go, like a bridge. They are talked about, sketched out, prototyped, played with, refactored, tuned, tested, tweaked, deleted, rewritten....

A program is not built; it is grown.

Because a program is always growing and always changing, it must be written with change in mind. I know it's not really clear yet what this means in practical terms, but I'll be bringing it up throughout the book.

Probably the first, most basic rule of good programming is to avoid duplication of code at all costs. This is sometimes called the DRY rule: Don't Repeat Yourself.

I usually think of it in another way: a good programmer cultivates the virtue of laziness. (But not just any laziness. You must be aggressively, proactively lazy!) Save yourself work whenever possible. If making a few changes now means you'll be able to save yourself more work later, do it! Make your program a place where you can do the absolute minimum amount of work to get the job done. Not only is programming this way much more interesting (it's very boring to do the same thing over and over and over...), but it produces less buggy code, and it produces it faster. It's a win-win-win situation.

Either way you look at it (DRY or laziness), the idea is the same: make your programs flexible. When change comes (and it *always* does), you'll have a much easier time changing with it.

Well, that about wraps it up. Looking at other technical books I own, they always seem to have a section here about "Who should read this book" or "How to read this book" or something. Well...I think *you* should read it, and front-to-back always works for me. (I mean, I did put the chapters in this order for a reason, you know.) Anyway, I never read that crap, so let's program!

## CHAPTER 1

Getting Started

We'll be using three main tools when we program: a text editor (to write your programs), the Ruby interpreter (to run your programs), and your command line (which is how you tell your computer which programs you want to run).

Although there's pretty much just one Ruby interpreter and one command line, there are many text editors to choose from—and some are much better for programming than others. A good text editor can help catch many of those "stupid mistakes" that beginner programmers make...oh, all right, that *all* programmers make. It makes your code much easier for yourself and others to read in a number of ways: by helping with indentation and formatting, by letting you set markers in your code (so you can easily return to something you are working on), by helping you match up your parentheses, and most important by *syntax coloring* (coloring different parts of your code with different colors according to their meanings in the program). You'll see syntax coloring in the examples in this book.

With so many good editors (and so many bad ones), it can be hard to know which to choose. I'll tell you which ones I use, though; that will have to be good enough for now. But whatever you choose as your text editor, do *not* use a word processor! Aside from being made for an entirely different purpose, they usually don't produce plain text, and your code must be in plain text for your programs to run.

Since setting up your environment differs somewhat from platform to platform (which text editors are available, how to install Ruby, how your command line works...), we'll look at setting up each platform covered in this book, one at a time.

1.1 Windows

First, let's install Ruby. Go get the One-Click Installer from the website (http://rubyinstaller.org/) by clicking Download and then clicking the highest-numbered version of Ruby you see there (version 1.9.2 as of this writing). When you run it, it will ask you where you want to install Ruby and which parts of it you want installed. Just accept all the defaults.

Now let's make a folder on your desktop in which you'll keep all of your programs. Right-click your desktop, select New, and then select Folder. Name it something truly memorable, such as programs. Now double-click the folder to open it.

To make a blank Ruby program, right-click in the folder, select New, and then select Text Document. Rename the document to have the .rb file extension. So if it was "New Text Document.txt", rename it to "ponies.rb" (if your program was about ponies).

Now, when you installed Ruby, you also installed a really nice text editor called SciTE (which is what I use when I'm on Windows or Linux). To use it to edit your new program, right-click your program, and select Edit. (When you get to the next chapter, you'll even write a program here, but for now let's just wait.)

To actually run your programs, you'll need to go to your command line. In your Start menu, select Accessories, and then choose Command Prompt. You'll see something like this:

Now some of you overachievers may have noticed that you can run your programs straight from SciTE by pressing F5. However, this *will not work* for any but the simplest of programs. You *will* need to use the command line, so you might as well get used to it now.

```
Microsoft Windows XP [Version 5.1.2600]
(C) Copyright 1985-2001 Microsoft Corp.

C:\Documents and Settings\chris>_
```

(That cursor at the end will probably be blinking; it's your computer's way of asking, "What would you like?")

So, here we are, at the command line, which is your direct connection to the soul of your computer. You want to be somewhat careful way down here, since it's not *too* hard to do Bad Things (things such as erase everything on your computer). But if you don't try anything too wacky, you should be fine.

Boy, when I was a kid, all we had was the command line! None of these fancy buttons or mice. We typed! Up hill! In the driving snow! And we liked it!

So, here you are, basically just staring at your computer naked. It would only be polite to say "hello" at this point, so type *echo hello* on the command line, and press Enter. Your computer should reply with a friendly hello as well, making your screen look something like this:

```
C:\Documents and Settings\chris> echo hello
hello

C:\Documents and Settings\chris>_
```

And your cursor is blinking again in a "What's next?" sort of way. Now that you're acquainted, ask it to make sure Ruby is installed properly and to tell you the version number. We do this with *ruby -v*:

```
C:\Documents and Settings\chris> ruby -v
ruby 1.9.2p180 (2011-02-18) [i386-mingw32]

C:\Documents and Settings\chris>_
```

Great! All we have left now is to find your programs folder through your command line. It's on your desktop, so we need to go there first. We do this with *cd desktop*:

```
C:\Documents and Settings\chris> cd desktop

C:\Documents and Settings\chris\Desktop>_
```

So, now we see what the C:\Documents and Settings\chris was all about. That's where we were on the command line. But now we're on the desktop (or C:\Documents and Settings\chris\Desktop according to the computer).

Why *cd*? Well, way back in the olden days, before CDs (when people were getting down to eight-track cassettes and phonographs and such) and when command lines roamed the earth in their terrible splendor, people didn't call them *folders* on your computer. After all, there were no pictures of folders (since this was before people had discovered crayons and Photoshop), so people didn't think of them as folders. They called them *directories*. So, they didn't "move from folder to folder." They "changed directories." But if you actually try typing *change_directory desktop* all day long, you barely have time to get down to your funky eight-track cassettes; so, it was shortened to just *cd*.

If you want to go back up a directory, you use *cd ..*:

```
C:\Documents and Settings\chris\Desktop> cd ..

C:\Documents and Settings\chris>_
```

And to see all the directories you can *cd* into from where you are, use *dir /ad*:

```
C:\Documents and Settings\chris> dir /ad
 Volume in drive C is System
 Volume Serial Number is 843D-8EDC

 Directory of C:\Documents and Settings\chris
```

```
07.10.2005  14:30    <DIR>              .
07.10.2005  14:30    <DIR>              ..
02.09.2005  10:45    <DIR>              Application Data
04.10.2005  16:19    <DIR>              Cookies
07.10.2005  14:24    <DIR>              Desktop
15.08.2005  13:17    <DIR>              Favorites
10.02.2005  02:50    <DIR>              Local Settings
05.09.2005  13:17    <DIR>              My Documents
15.08.2005  14:14    <DIR>              NetHood
10.02.2005  02:50    <DIR>              PrintHood
07.10.2005  15:23    <DIR>              Recent
10.02.2005  02:50    <DIR>              SendTo
10.02.2005  02:50    <DIR>              Start Menu
25.02.2005  14:57    <DIR>              Templates
25.02.2005  12:07    <DIR>              UserData
              0 File(s)              0 bytes
             15 Dir(s)   6 720 483 328 bytes free

C:\Documents and Settings\chris>_
```

And there you go!

1.2 Mac OS X

If you're using OS X, you're in luck! You can use the best (in my opinion) text editor, Ruby is already installed for you in OS X 10.2 (Jaguar) and up, and you get to use a real command line (not that silly wanna-be command line we have to use on Windows)!

My absolute favorite editor is TextMate (http://macromates.com/). It's cute, it's sweet, and it has great Ruby support. The only drawback is that it's not free. But if you code as much as I do, it's worth the (fairly cheap) price. And if you're using a Mac, then I assume you are accustomed to getting the best...and paying for it! In any case, it has a fully functional free trial, so you can give it a try if you want. If you really need a free text editor, though, try TextWrangler (http://www.barebones.com/products/textwrangler/). It gets the job done.

If you decide to go with the built-in TextEdit editor (which I do *not* advise), make sure you save your programs as plain text! (Select Make Plain Text from the Format menu.) Otherwise, your programs *will not* work.

Next, you should make a folder on your desktop in which to keep your programs. Right-click (oops! I mean Ctrl-click) on your desktop, and select New Folder. You want to give it a name both descriptive and alluring, such as programs. Nice.

Now, let's get to know your computer a little better. The best way to really have a one-on-one with your computer is on the command line. You get there through the Terminal application (found in the Finder by navigating to Applications/Utilities). Open it, and you'll see something like this:

```
Last login: Sat Oct  8 12:05:33 on ttyp1
Welcome to Darwin!
mezzaluna:~ chris$ _
```

(That cursor at the end might be blinking, and it might be a vertical line instead of an underscore. Whatever it looks like, it's your computer's way of asking "What would you like?")

It's telling me when I last logged in (though if it's your first time, it might not say that), welcoming me to Darwin (the deep, dark internals of OS X), and giving me a *command prompt* and cursor. Prompts, like West-Coast hairdos, come in a variety of shapes, sizes, colors, and levels of expressivity. This isn't the prompt I normally use (nor is this the hairdo I normally use—I think this is the first time I've worn pigtails out of the house), but it's the default prompt. It's showing the name of this computer ("mezzaluna"), what two dots look like (":"), something else I'll tell you about in just a bit ("~"), who I am ("chris"), and then just a dollar sign ("$"). This is for good luck, I guess. Maybe it's trying to give my name a little bling bling. I don't know.

Anyway, here we are, at the command line, which is the heart and soul of your computer. You want to be somewhat careful what you do down here, since it's not *too* hard to do Bad Things here. (It's easier to delete everything on your computer than it is to get rid of that dollar sign, for example.) But if you don't try anything too rambunctious, you should be fine.

Here you are, basically just staring at your computer naked. It would only be polite to say "hello" at this point, so type *echo hello* on the command line, and press Return . Your computer should reply with a friendly hello as well, making your screen look something like this:

```
mezzaluna:~ chris$ echo hello
hello
mezzaluna:~ chris$ _
```

And your cursor is blinking again in a "What's next?" sort of way. Now that you're acquainted, ask your computer whether it has Ruby installed and, if so, which version. Do this with *ruby -v*:

```
mezzaluna:~ chris$ ruby -v
ruby 1.9.2p180 (2011-02-18) [universal-darwin9.0]
```

That's good—I have Ruby 1.9.2 installed. But 1.8.*anything* is pretty good. If you have an earlier version, you can still use it, but a few examples in this book might not do exactly the same thing for you. (Almost everything should work, though.)

Now that Ruby is ready to rumble, it's time to learn how to get around your computer from the command line and what that ~ in the prompt is all about.

The ~ is just a short way of saying "your home directory," which is just a geek way of saying "your default folder," which is still kind of geeky anyway. And I'm OK with that.

That's where you are: your home directory. If you want to change to a different directory, you use *cd*. (No one wants to type *change-directory*, not even once. I mean, I had to just then, to make a point, but in general you really don't want to type it.)

```
mezzaluna:~ chris$ cd Desktop
mezzaluna:~/Desktop chris$ _
```

So, my prompt changed, telling me that I'm now on my desktop, which is itself in my home directory. (Notice that *Desktop* was capitalized. If you don't capitalize it, your computer will get angry and begin to swear at you in computerese, with such insults as "No such" and "file" and the worst one of all: "bash.") You can go back up a directory with *cd ..*, which in this case would put you back in your home directory. And at any time, if you just type *cd* by itself, that takes you to your home directory, no matter where you are. This is just like the Return spell in Dragon Warrior (the original Dragon Warrior; I don't play any of these new-fangled "fun" versions…).

But we don't want either of those. We want to go to your programs folder (or directory, or whatever). Assuming you're still in your Desktop folder (if not, get there quick!), just do this:

```
mezzaluna:~/Desktop chris$ cd programs
mezzaluna:~/Desktop/programs chris$ _
```

But you probably could have guessed that.

As they say here in Norway: "Bra!" (See why I like it here? I'm not even allowed to tell you what they say for "five" and "six.") Now you're ready to program.

1.3 Linux

If you're using Linux, you probably already have a favorite text editor, you know how to install Ruby with your package manager, and you better already know where to find your command line.

If you don't have a text editor you're fond of, though, might I recommend SciTE? It's made specifically for programming, it plays well with Ruby, and it's free. You can download it from http://www.scintilla.org/SciTE.html. If you use another relatively popular editor (emacs, vim, and so on), you can probably find Ruby syntax highlighting rules and such for it.

Next, you'll want to see whether you have Ruby installed already. Type *which ruby* on your command line. If you see a scary-looking message that looks something like /usr/bin/which: no ruby in (...), then you'll need to install it. Otherwise, see what version of Ruby you are running with *ruby -v*. If it is 1.8.7 or older, then you might want to upgrade.

If you're using Ubuntu, you can use the Synaptic Package Manager to install or upgrade to the latest stable version of Ruby. You'll find it in the Main menu in the System/Administration group. (On other Linux distributions you'll want to use whatever is your default package manager, of course, but the general idea is the same.)

In Synaptic Package Manager, search for *ruby*. A bunch of Ruby-related packages will show up; find and install the package named simply *ruby*. That's it.

Run one final *ruby -v*, just to make sure the gods are still smiling on you:

```
$ruby -v
ruby 1.9.2p180 (2011-02-18) [i486-linux]
```

Perfect! Now all that's left is to create a directory somewhere to keep your programs in, *cd* into that directory, and you're all set!

All right! Are you ready? Take a deep breath. Let's program!

## CHAPTER 2

Numbers

Now that you've gotten everything ready, it's time to write your first program! Open your text editor, and type the following:

```
puts 1+2
```

Save your program (yep, that's a complete program!) as calc.rb. Now run your program by typing *ruby calc.rb* into your command line. It should put a 3 on your screen. See, programming isn't so hard, now is it?

2.1 Did It Work?

If it worked, that's great. But I get a lot of emails from people who are stuck right here. Did you see a window flash up and then disappear? Or nothing at all? If so, the problem is probably that you didn't run your program from the command line.

Don't just click your program's icon.

Don't just press F5 in your text editor.

Run it by typing *ruby calc.rb* into your command line. Trust me.

2.2 Introduction to puts

So, what's going on in that program? I'm sure you can guess what the 1+2 does; our program is basically the same as this:

```
puts 3
```

puts simply writes onto the screen whatever comes after it.

2.3   Integer and Float

In most programming languages (and Ruby is no exception), numbers without decimal points are called *integers*, and numbers with decimal points are usually called *floating-point numbers* or, more simply, *floats*.

Here are some integers:

```
5
-205
999999999999999999999999
0
```

And here are some floats:

```
54.321
0.001
-205.3884
0.0
```

In practice, most programs don't use floats; they use only integers. (After all, no one wants to look at 7.4 emails, browse 1.8 web pages, or listen to 5.24 of their favorite songs.) Floats are used more for academic purposes (physics experiments and such) and for audio and video (including 3D) programs. Even most money programs use integers; they just keep track of the number of pennies!

2.4   Simple Arithmetic

So far, we have all the makings of a simple calculator. (Calculators always use floats, so if you want your computer to act just like a calculator, you should also use floats.) You type numbers using the digit keys (either at the top of your keyboard or on the numeric keypad). For decimal points, you use the period (or full-stop, normally close to the M key on the bottom row or over on the numeric keypad). Don't, however, type commas into your numbers. If you enter 1,000,000, you'll just confuse Ruby.

For addition and subtraction, we use + and - , as we saw. For multiplication, we use * , and for division we use / . Most keyboards have these keys in the numeric keypad on the far-right side, but you can also use Shift 8 and / (the same key as the ? key). Let's try to expand our calc.rb program a little. Try coding this program:

```
puts 1.0 + 2.0
puts 2.0 * 3.0
puts 5.0 - 8.0
puts 9.0 / 2.0
```

This is what the program returns:

```
3.0
6.0
-3.0
4.5
```

(The spaces in the program are not important; they just make the code easier to read.) Well, that wasn't too surprising. Now let's try it with integers:

```
puts 1+2
puts 2*3
puts 5-8
puts 9/2
```

This is mostly the same, right?

```
3
6
-3
4
```

Uh…except for that last one! When you do arithmetic with integers, you'll get integer answers. When your computer can't get the "right" answer, it always rounds down. (Of course, 4 *is* the right answer in integer arithmetic for 9/2. It just might not be the answer you were expecting.)

Perhaps you're wondering what integer division is good for. Well, let's say you're going to the movies but you have only $9. When I lived in Portland a few years back, you could see a movie at the Bagdad for two bucks. (It was cheaper for two people to go to the Bagdad and get a pitcher of beer, *good* beer, than to go see a movie at your typical theater. And the seats all had tables in front of them! For your beer! It was heavenly!) Anyway, nostalgia aside, how many movies could you see at the Bagdad for nine bucks? 9/2…4 movies. You can see that 4.5 is definitely *not* the right answer in this case; they will not let you watch half of a movie or let half of you in to see a whole movie…some things just aren't divisible.

So, now experiment with some programs of your own! If you want to write more complex expressions, you can use parentheses. For example:

```
puts 5 * (12-8) + -15
puts 98 + (59872 / (13*8)) * -51
```

```
5
-29227
```

2.5 A Few Things to Try

Write a program that tells you the following:

- *Hours in a year.* How many hours are in a year?

- *Minutes in a decade.* How many minutes are in a decade?

- *Your age in seconds.* How many seconds old are you? (I'm not going to check your answer, so be as accurate—or not—as you want.)

Here's a tougher question:

- *Our dear author's age.* If I am 1,111 million seconds old (which I am, though I was somewhere in the 800 millions when I started this book), how old am I?

## CHAPTER 3

Letters

We've learned all about numbers, but what about letters? Words? Text?

We refer to groups of letters in a program as *strings*. (You can think of beads with letters on them being strung together.) To make it easier to see just what part of the code is in a string, I'll color strings 'blue'. Here are some strings:

```
'Hello.'
'Ruby rocks.'
'Nobody deserves a mime, Buffy.'
'Snoopy says #%^?&*@! when he stubs his toe.'
'         '
''
```

As you can see, strings can have punctuation, digits, symbols, and spaces in them...more than just letters. That last string doesn't have anything in it at all; we call that an *empty string*.

We used puts to print numbers; let's try it with some strings:

```
puts 'Hello, world!'
puts ''
puts 'Good-bye.'
```

```
Hello, world!

Good-bye.
```

Dig it.

3.1 String Arithmetic

Just as you can do arithmetic on numbers, you can also do arithmetic on strings! Well, sort of...you can add strings, anyway. Let's try to add two strings and see what puts does with that:

```
puts 'I like' + 'apple pie.'
```

```
I likeapple pie.
```

Snap! I forgot to put a space between 'I like' and 'apple pie.'. Spaces don't usually matter much in your code, but they matter inside strings. (You know what they say: computers don't do what you *want* them to do, only what you *tell* them to do.) Take two:

```
puts 'I like ' + 'apple pie.'
puts 'I like' + ' apple pie.'
```

```
I like apple pie.
I like apple pie.
```

(As you can see, it didn't matter to which string I added the space.)

So, you can add strings, but you can also multiply them! (And I know you wanted to...you were all like, "But, Chris, can we multiply them?" Yes. Yes, you can.) Watch this:

```
puts 'blink ' * 4
```

And you get this:

```
batting her eyes
```

(Just kidding...not even Ruby is that clever.)

```
blink blink blink blink
```

If you think about it, this makes perfect sense. After all, 7*3 really just means 7+7+7, so 'moo'*3 just means 'moo'+'moo'+'moo'.

3.2   12 vs. '12'

Before we get any further, we should make sure we understand the difference between *numbers* and *digits*. 12 is a number, but '12' is a string of two digits.

Let's play around with this for a while:

```
puts  12  +  12
puts '12' + '12'
puts '12  +  12'
```

```
24
1212
12  +  12
```

How about this?

```
puts  2  *  5
puts '2' *  5
puts '2  *  5'
```

```
10
22222
2  *  5
```

These examples are pretty clear. However, if you're not too careful with how you mix your strings and your numbers, you might run into…

3.3 Problems

At this point you may have tried some things that *didn't* work. If not, here are a few:

```
puts '12' + 12
puts '2' * '5'
```

```
#<TypeError: can't convert Fixnum into String>
```

Hmmm…an error message. The problem is that you can't really add a number to a string or multiply a string by another string. It doesn't make any more sense than this does:

```
puts 'Betty' + 12
puts 'Fred' * 'John'
```

Here's something else to be aware of: you can write 'pig'*5 in a program, since it just means five sets of the string 'pig' all added together. However, you *can't* write 5*'pig', since that means 'pig' sets of the number 5, which is…poetic, at best.

Finally, what if we want a program to print out You're swell!? We can try this:

```
puts 'You're swell!'
```

Well, *that* won't work; I can tell that just from the syntax coloring. I won't even try to run it. The problem is that your computer can't tell the difference between an apostrophe and a single quote (to end the string). I think the confusion is reasonable here, though. They are the same character, after all. We need a way to tell the computer "I want an apostrophe here, inside this string." How do we let the computer know we want to stay in the string? We have to *escape* the apostrophe, like this:

Why is this called *escaping*? I have no idea—maybe because we are escaping from the normal way of doing things? Yeah, that's a bit of a stretch. But whatever the reason, that's what programmers call it, so that's what we'll call it.

```
puts 'You\'re swell!'
```

```
You're swell!
```

The backslash is the escape character. In other words, if you have a backslash and another character, they are sometimes translated into a new character. The only things the backslash escapes, though, are the apostrophe and the backslash itself. (If you think about it, escape characters must always escape themselves, too, to allow for the construction of any string. Why is that?)

Let's see a few examples of escaping in strings:

```
puts 'You\'re swell!'
puts 'backslash at the end of a string:  \\'
puts 'up\\down'
puts 'up\down'
```

```
You're swell!
backslash at the end of a string:  \
up\down
up\down
```

Since the backslash does *not* escape a d but *does* escape itself, those last two strings are identical. Obviously they don't look the same in the code, but when your program is actually running, those are just two ways of describing identical strings.

You good so far? Good. Let's start doing something slightly more clever....

## CHAPTER 4

Variables and Assignment

So far, whenever we have putsed a string or a number, the thing we putsed is gone. What I mean is, if we wanted to print something out twice, we would have to type it in twice:

```
puts '...you can say that again...'
puts '...you can say that again...'
```

```
...you can say that again...
...you can say that again...
```

It would be nice if we could just type it in once and then hang on to it...store it somewhere. Well, we can, of course. It would have been insensitive to bring it up otherwise.

To store the string in your computer's memory for use later in your program, you need to give the string a name. Programmers often refer to this process as *assignment*, and they call the names *variables*. A variable name can usually be just about any sequence of letters and numbers, but in Ruby the first character of this name needs to be a lowercase letter. Let's try that last program again, but this time I will give the string the name my_string (though I could just as well have named it str or myOwnLittleString or henry_the_8th):

```
my_string = '...you can say that again...'
puts my_string
puts my_string
```

```
...you can say that again...
...you can say that again...
```

Whenever you tried to do something to my_string, the program did it to '...you can say that again...' instead. You can think of the variable my_string as "pointing to" the string '...you can say that again...'. Here's a slightly more motivated example:

Sure, sure, we could copy and paste that line, but that is not maximally lazy: what if we want to change one of those lines at some point in the future? We don't want to have to change *anything* twice. Copy and paste is the opposite of "Don't Repeat Yourself."

So, is this program prettier than the first example? Yes. This is longer but prettier. We'll make it prettier still, and even shorter than the original, on page 54. Beautiful....

```
name = 'Anya Christina Emmanuella Jenkins Harris'
puts 'My name is ' + name + '.'
puts 'Wow!  ' + name
puts 'is a really long name!'
```

```
My name is Anya Christina Emmanuella Jenkins Harris.
Wow!  Anya Christina Emmanuella Jenkins Harris
is a really long name!
```

My wife made me put in the Harris.

Also, just as we can *assign* an object to a variable, we can *reassign* a different object to that variable. (This is why we call them *variables*—what they point to can vary.)

```
composer = 'Mozart'
puts composer + ' was "da bomb" in his day.'

composer = 'Beethoven'
puts 'But I prefer ' + composer + ', personally.'
```

```
Mozart was "da bomb" in his day.
But I prefer Beethoven, personally.
```

Of course, variables can point to any kind of object, not just strings:

```
my_own_var = 'just another ' + 'string'
puts my_own_var

my_own_var = 5 * (1+2)
puts my_own_var
```

```
just another string
15
```

In fact, variables can point to just about anything...except other variables. So, what happens if we try the following?

```
var1 = 8
var2 = var1
puts var1
puts var2

puts ''

var1 = 'eight'
puts var1
puts var2
```

```
8
8

eight
8
```

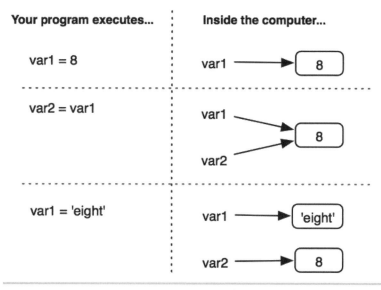

Figure 1—Variables point to values

On the second line, when we tried to point var2 to var1, it really pointed to 8 instead (just like var1 was pointing to). Then on the eighth line, we had var1 point to the string 'eight', but since var2 was never really pointing at var1, it stays pointing at the *number* 8. If you like to think about these things visually, it might help to look at the figure *Variables point to values*.

## CHAPTER 5

Mixing It Up

We've looked at a few kinds of objects (integers, floats, and strings), and we made variables point to them. Now it's time for them all to play nicely together.

We've seen that if we want a program to print 25, the following *does not work*, because you can't add numbers and strings together:

```
var1 = 2
var2 = '5'
puts var1 + var2
```

Part of the problem is that your computer doesn't know if you were trying to get 7 (2 + 5) or if you wanted to get 25 ('2' + '5'). But we'll learn how to do both.

Before we can add these together, we need some way of getting the string version of var1 or of getting the integer version of var2.

5.1 Conversions

To get the string version of an object, we simply write .to_s after it:

```
var1 = 2
var2 = '5'
puts var1.to_s + var2
```

```
25
```

Similarly, .to_i gives the integer version of an object, and .to_f gives the float version. Let's look at what these three methods do (and *don't* do) a little more closely:

```
var1 = 2
var2 = '5'
puts var1.to_s + var2
puts var1 + var2.to_i
```

```
25
7
```

Notice that, even after we got the string version of var1 by calling to_s, var1 was always pointing at 2 and never at '2'. Unless we explicitly reassign var1 (which requires an = sign), it will point at 2 for the life of the program.

Now let's try some more interesting (and a few just weird) conversions:

```
Line 1  puts '15'.to_f
     2  puts '99.999'.to_f
     3  puts '99.999'.to_i
     4  puts ''
     5  puts '5 is my favorite number!'.to_i
     6  puts 'Who asked you about 5 or whatever?'.to_i
     7  puts 'Your momma did.'.to_f
     8  puts ''
     9  puts 'stringy'.to_s
    10  puts 3.to_i
```

```
15.0
99.999
99

5
0
0.0

stringy
3
```

So, this probably gave you some surprises. The first one is pretty standard, giving 15.0. After that, we converted the string '99.999' to a float and to an integer. The float did what we expected; the integer was, as always, rounded down.

Next, we had some examples of some...*unusual* strings being converted into numbers. On line 5, to_i ignores the first thing it doesn't understand (and the rest of the string from that point on). So, the first one was converted to 5, but the others, since they started with letters, were ignored completely, so the computer just picks zero.

Finally, we saw that our last two conversions did nothing at all, just as we would expect.

5.2 Another Look at puts

There's something strange about our favorite method. Take a look at this:

```
puts  20
puts  20.to_s
puts '20'
```

```
20
20
20
```

Why do these three all print the same thing? Well, the last two should, since 20.to_s is '20'. But what about the first one, the integer 20? For that matter, what does it even mean to write *the integer* 20? When you write a *2* and then a *0* on a piece of paper, you are writing a string, not an integer. The integer 20 is the number of fingers and toes I have; it isn't a *2* followed by a *0*.

Well, here's the big secret behind our friend puts: before puts tries to write out an object, it uses to_s to get the string version of that object. In fact, the *s* in puts stands for *string*; puts really means *put string*.

This may not seem too exciting now, but Ruby has many, *many* kinds of objects (you'll even learn how to make your own), and it's nice to know what will happen if you try to puts a really weird object, such as a picture of your grandmother or a music file or something. It'll always be converted to a string first. But that will come later. In the meantime, we have a few more methods for you, and they allow us to write all sorts of fun programs.

5.3 The gets Method

If puts means *put string*, I'm sure you can guess what gets stands for. And just as puts always spits out strings, gets retrieves only strings. And whence does it get them?

From you! Well, from your keyboard, anyway. And since your keyboard makes only strings, that works out beautifully. What actually happens is that gets just sits there, reading what you type until you press Enter . Let's try it:

```
puts gets
```

```
⇒ Is there an echo in here?
‹ Is there an echo in here?
```

Of course, whatever you type will just get repeated back to you. Run it a few times, and try typing different things.

5.4 Did It Work?

Maybe you didn't need any help installing Ruby, so you skipped Chapter 1. No problem.

Maybe you've done a little programming before, so you skipped Chapter 2. That's fine.

The only thing is that you missed some stuff there that you didn't *really* need until now. If you haven't been running your programs from the command line, then you'll almost certainly have problems with gets, and we're going to be using it a lot from now on. So, if you saved your program as example.rb, you should really run your program by typing *ruby example.rb* into your command line. If you're having trouble getting around on your command line, check out Chapter 1, *Getting Started*, on page 1.

5.5 The chomp Method

Excitement! Now we can make interactive programs! In this one, type your name, and it will greet you:

```
puts 'Hello there, and what\'s your name?'
name = gets
puts 'Your name is ' + name + '?  What a lovely name!'
puts 'Pleased to meet you, ' + name + '.  :)'
```

Eek! I just ran it—I typed my name, and this is what happened:

```
‹ Hello there, and what's your name?
⇒ Chris
‹ Your name is Chris
  ?  What a lovely name!
  Pleased to meet you, Chris
  .  :)
```

Hmmm...it looks like when I typed the letters `C`, `h`, `r`, `i`, and `s` and then pressed `Enter`, gets got all the letters in my name *and* the `Enter`! Fortunately, there's a method that deals with just this sort of thing: chomp. It takes off any `Enter` characters hanging out at the end of your string. Let's try that program again, but with chomp to help us this time:

```
puts 'Hello there, and what\'s your name?'
name = gets.chomp
puts 'Your name is ' + name + '?  What a lovely name!'
puts 'Pleased to meet you, ' + name + '.  :)'
```

```
‹ Hello there, and what's your name?
⇒ Chris
‹ Your name is Chris?  What a lovely name!
  Pleased to meet you, Chris.  :)
```

Much better! Notice that since name is pointing to gets.chomp, we don't ever have to say name.chomp; name was already chomped. (Of course, if we did chomp it again, it wouldn't do anything; it has no more `Enter` characters to chomp off.

We could chomp on that string all day, and it wouldn't change it. Like week-old bubble gum.)

5.6 A Few Things to Try

- *Full name greeting.* Write a program that asks for a person's first name, then middle, and then last. Finally, it should greet the person using their full name.

- *Bigger, better favorite number.* Write a program that asks for a person's favorite number. Have your program add 1 to the number, and then suggest the result as a bigger and better favorite number. (Do be tactful about it, though.)

5.7 Mind Your Variables

When writing a program, I always try to have a good feel for what each variable is pointing to: a number, a string, or whatever. Like in the favorite number program, at some point you'll have the person's favorite number as a string, and at another point you'll have it as an integer. It's important to keep track of which is which, and you can do this by keeping them in different variables.

And name the variables so it's easy to tell what they are at a glance. If I had a variable for someone's name, I might call it name, and I would just assume it was a string. If I had someone's age in a variable, I might call it age, and I'd assume it was an integer. So if I needed to have the string version of someone's age, I'd try to make that obvious by calling it something like age_string or age_as_string.

I'm not sure you know, but this book started out as an online tutorial. (It was much shorter back then.) I've gotten hundreds of emails from people getting stuck. In most of those cases, the problem was a conversion problem. And usually, it was just someone trying to add an integer and a string together. Let's look at that error a bit more closely:

```
my_birth_month = 'August'
my_birth_day   = 3

puts my_birth_month + my_birth_day
```

```
#<TypeError: can't convert Fixnum into String>
```

What is this error telling us? First, what's a *Fixnum*? Basically, it's an integer. For performance reasons, given the way computers are built and such, there are two different classes of integers in Ruby: Fixnums and Bignums. Basically, really big integers are Bignums, and smaller ones are Fixnums. You don't really need to know this, though; all you need to know is that when you see Fixnum or Bignum, you know it's an integer.

Most programming languages don't have anything like Bignum (at least not built in), so all of your integers have to be relatively small, and if you add two largish integers, you might end up with a very small one or even a negative one. Blech.

So, it can't convert an integer into a string. Well, you know it *can* convert an integer into a string, but it doesn't want to without your explicit instructions. (Eh…it's only a computer, after all, and computers aren't exactly known for their independent thinking and initiative.) Honestly, it's probably a good thing, because maybe you don't want to convert the integer into a string, you know? Maybe you want to convert the string into an integer. It's the whole "2 plus 5 adding up to 7 or 25" problem we covered on page 21.

It's easy to get frustrated when your program has errors. I try not to think of them as errors, though. I try to think of them as the pathetic attempts of a socially inept non-native English speaker (your computer) asking for help. If only your computer were a bit more cultured, it might say something more like, "Excuse me, but I'm unclear as to just one small point…did you want me to convert the integer to a string here, or vice versa? Although it's probably obvious to any human what you are trying to do, I'm just not that bright." Then it would laugh nervously. Someday our computers will do just that, but in the meantime, pity the poor fool.

## CHAPTER 6

More About Methods

So far we've seen a number of different methods—puts, gets, and so on. (Pop quiz: List all the methods we have seen so far! There are ten of them; the answer is below.) However, we haven't really talked about what methods are.

I believe the technical definition is that "methods are things that do stuff." If objects (such as strings, integers, and floats) are the nouns in the Ruby language, then methods are like the verbs. And, just like in English, you can't have a verb without a noun to *do* the verb. For example, ticking isn't something that just happens; a clock (biological or otherwise) has to do it. In English, we would say "The clock ticks." In Ruby we would say clock.tick (assuming that clock was a Ruby object, of course, and one that could tick). Programmers might say we were "calling clock's tick method" or that we "called tick on clock." (This goes a long way toward explaining why we aren't invited to many parties. We? *They!* Why *they* aren't invited to many parties....)

Anyway, did you take the quiz? Good. Well, I'm sure you remembered the methods puts, gets, and chomp, since we just covered those. You probably also got our conversion methods, to_i, to_f, and to_s. But did you get the other four? Yeah? No? Why, it's none other than our old arithmetic buddies: +, -, *, and /! (See, it's stuff like that. Arithmetic buddies? Seriously, Chris?)

As I was saying, just as every verb needs a noun, every method needs an object. It's usually easy to tell which object is performing the method. It's what comes right before the dot, like in our clock.tick example or in 101.to_s. Sometimes, though, it's not quite as obvious, as with the arithmetic methods. As it turns out, 5 + 5 is really just a shortcut way of writing 5.+ 5. For example:

```
puts('hello '.+ 'world')
puts((10.* 9).+ 9)
```

```
hello world
99
```

It isn't very pretty, so we won't ever write it like that; however, it's important to understand what is *really* happening.

This also gives us a deeper understanding of why we can do 'pig'*5 but we can't do 5*'pig': 'pig'*5 is telling 'pig' to do the multiplying, but 5*'pig' is telling 5 to do the multiplying. 'pig' knows how to make 5 copies of itself and add them all together; however, 5 will have a much more difficult time of making 'pig' copies of *itself* and adding them together.

And, of course, we still have puts and gets to explain. Where are their objects? In English, you can sometimes leave out the noun; for example, if a villain yells "Die!" the implicit noun is whomever he is yelling at. In Ruby, if I say puts 'to be or not to be', the implicit object is whatever object you happen to be *in*. But we don't even know *how* to be in an object yet; we've always been inside a special object Ruby has created for us that represents the whole program. You can always see what object you are in by using the special variable self. Watch this:

```
puts self
```

```
main
```

If you didn't entirely follow all of that, that's OK. The important thing to get from all this is that every method is being done by some object, even if it doesn't have a dot in front of it. If you understand that, then you're all set.

6.1 Fancy String Methods

Let's learn a few fun string methods. You don't have to memorize them all; you can just look up this page again if you forget them. I just want to show you a *small* part of what strings can do. In fact, I can't remember even half of the string methods myself—but that's fine, because you can find great references on the Internet with all the string methods listed and explained. (I will show you where to find them in Chapter 15, *Beyond This Fine Book*, on page 123.) Really, I don't even *want* to know all the string methods; it's kind of like knowing every word in the dictionary. I can speak English just fine without knowing every word in the dictionary. (And isn't that really the whole point of the dictionary? You don't *have* to know what's in it.)

Our first string method is reverse, which returns a reversed version of the string:

FF1 SPOILER ALERT! (From back when *final* used to mean something.)

```
var1 = 'stop'
var2 = 'deliver repaid desserts'
var3 = '....TCELES B HSUP  A magic spell?'
```

```
puts var1.reverse
puts var2.reverse
puts var3.reverse
puts var1
puts var2
puts var3
```

```
pots
stressed diaper reviled
?lleps cigam A  PUSH B SELECT....
stop
deliver repaid desserts
....TCELES B HSUP  A magic spell?
```

As you can see, reverse doesn't change the original string; it just makes a new backward version of it. That's why var1 is still 'stop' even after we called reverse on it.

Another string method is length, which tells us the number of characters (including spaces) in the string:

```
puts 'What is your full name?'
name = gets.chomp
puts 'Did you know there are ' + name.length + ' characters'
puts 'in your name, ' + name + '?'
```

```
❮ What is your full name?
⇒ Christopher David Pine
❮ #<TypeError: can't convert Fixnum into String>
```

Uh-oh! See? There it is! It's an easy mistake to make. Anyway, if you didn't know to be on the lookout for this error, you can still figure that the problem must have happened sometime after the line name = gets.chomp, since I was able to type my name. See whether you can figure it out.

You probably think that I made that mistake on purpose, since I'm obviously such a fabulous programmer that I'm writing a book on it. You were thinking that, right? Well…never mind.

The problem is with length: it gives us an integer, but we want a string. That's easy enough; we'll just throw in a .to_s (and cross our fingers):

```
puts 'What is your full name?'
name = gets.chomp
puts 'Did you know there are ' + name.length.to_s + ' characters'
puts 'in your name, ' + name + '?'
```

```
❮ What is your full name?
⇒ Christopher David Pine
❮ Did you know there are 22 characters
  in your name, Christopher David Pine?
```

No, I did not know that. Note: 22 is the number of *characters* in my name, not the number of *letters* (count 'em). I guess we could write a program that asks for your first, middle, and last names individually and then adds those lengths together—hey, why don't you do that? Go ahead, I'll wait.

Did you do it? Right on.

Well, unless your name is Bjørn or Håvard, in which case you had some problems. Ruby is expecting only ASCII characters (basically the stuff you can type on an American keyboard—the *A* in ASCII stands for *American*). It is possible to use any character in any language, but it requires some extra work and is just more advanced than what we're going to cover.

So, a number of string methods can also change the case (uppercase and lowercase) of your string. upcase changes every lowercase letter to uppercase, and downcase changes every uppercase letter to lowercase. swapcase switches the case of every letter in the string, and finally, capitalize is just like downcase, except it switches the first character to uppercase (if it's a letter).

```
letters = 'aAbBcCdDeE'
puts letters.upcase
puts letters.downcase
puts letters.swapcase
puts letters.capitalize
puts ' a'.capitalize
puts letters
```

```
AABBCCDDEE
aabbccddee
AaBbCcDdEe
Aabbccddee
 a
aAbBcCdDeE
```

As you can see from the line puts ' a'.capitalize, the capitalize method capitalizes only the first *character*, not the first *letter*. Also, as we have seen before, throughout all of these method calls, letters remains unchanged. I don't mean to belabor the point, but it's important to understand. Some methods *do* change the associated object, but we haven't seen any yet, and we won't for some time.

The last of the fancy string methods we'll look at do visual formatting. The first, center, adds spaces to the beginning and end of the string to make it centered. However, just like you have to tell the puts method what you want it to print and you have to tell the + method what you want it to add, you have to tell the center method how wide you want your centered string to be.

So if I wanted to center the lines of a poem, I would do it like this:

```
line_width = 50
puts(                'Old Mother Hubbard'.center(line_width))
puts(                'Sat in her cupboard'.center(line_width))
puts(          'Eating her curds and whey,'.center(line_width))
puts(             'When along came a spider'.center(line_width))
puts(             'Who sat down beside her'.center(line_width))
puts('And scared her poor shoe dog away.'.center(line_width))
```

```
        Old Mother Hubbard
        Sat in her cupboard
     Eating her curds and whey,
      When along came a spider
      Who sat down beside her
And scared her poor shoe dog away.
```

I wanted to line up the .center line_width part, so I added those extra spaces before the strings. This is just because I think it is prettier that way. Programmers often have strong feelings about code aesthetics, and they often disagree about them. The more you program, the more you will come into your own style.

Hmmm...I don't think that's how that nursery rhyme goes, but I'm too lazy to look it up. Speaking of laziness, see how I stored the width of the poem in the variable line_width? This was so that if I want to go back later and make the poem wider, I have to change only the first line of the program, instead of every line that does centering. With a very long poem, this could save me a lot of time. That's the kind of laziness we want in our programs.

About that centering...you may have noticed that it isn't quite as beautiful as a word processor would have done. If you really want perfect centering (and maybe a nicer font), then you should just use a word processor. Ruby is a wonderful tool, but no tool is the right tool for *every* job.

The other two string-formatting methods we'll look at today are ljust and rjust, which stand for *left justify* and *right justify*. They are similar to center, except that they pad the string with spaces on the right and left sides, respectively. Let's take a look at all three in action:

```
line_width = 40
str = '--> text <--'
puts(str.ljust( line_width))
puts(str.center(line_width))
puts(str.rjust( line_width))
puts(str.ljust(line_width/2) + str.rjust(line_width/2))
```

```
--> text <--
              --> text <--
                          --> text <--
--> text <--              --> text <--
```

6.2 A Few Things to Try

- *Angry boss.* Write an angry boss program that rudely asks what you want. Whatever you answer, the angry boss should yell it back to you and then fire you. For example, if you type in *I want a raise*, it should yell back like this:

```
WHADDAYA MEAN "I WANT A RAISE"?!? YOU'RE FIRED!!
```

- *Table of contents.* Here's something for you to do in order to play around more with center, ljust, and rjust: write a program that will display a table of contents so that it looks like this:

```
                  Table of Contents

Chapter 1:  Getting Started             page  1
Chapter 2:  Numbers                     page  9
Chapter 3:  Letters                     page 13
```

6.3 Higher Math

(This section is optional. Some of it assumes a fair degree of mathematical knowledge. If you aren't interested, you can go straight to Chapter 7, Flow Control, on page 37, without any problems. However, a quick scan of this section might come in handy.)

There aren't nearly as many number methods as there are string methods (though I still don't know them all off the top of my head). Here we'll look at the rest of the arithmetic methods, a random number generator, and the Math object, with its trigonometric and transcendental methods.

6.4 More Arithmetic

The other two arithmetic methods are ** (exponentiation) and % (modulus). So if you want to say "five squared" in Ruby, you would write it as 5**2. You can also use floats for your exponent, so if you want the square root of 5, you could write 5**0.5. The modulus method gives you the remainder after division by a number. So, for example, if you divide 7 by 3, you get 2 with a remainder of 1. Let's see it working in a program:

Modulus, much like integer division, might seem bizarre, but it is actually really useful, often when used with integer division.

```
puts 5**2
puts 5**0.5
puts 7/3
puts 7%3
puts 365%7
```

```
25
2.23606797749979
2
1
1
```

From that last line, we learn that a (nonleap) year has some number of weeks, plus one day. So if your birthday was on a Tuesday this year, it will be on a Wednesday next year. You can also use floats with the modulus method. Basically, it works the only sensible way it could...but I'll let you play around with that.

I have one last method to mention before we check out the random number generator: abs. This method simply returns the absolute value of the number:

```
puts (5-2).abs
puts (2-5).abs
```

```
3
3
```

6.5 Random Numbers

Ruby comes with a pretty nice random number generator. The method to get a randomly chosen number is rand. If you call rand just like that, you'll get a float greater than or equal to 0.0 and less than 1.0. If you give it an integer parameter (by calling rand(5), for example), it will give you an integer greater than or equal to 0 and less than 5 (so five possible numbers, from 0 to 4).

Let's see rand in action:

```
puts rand
puts rand
puts rand
puts(rand(100))
puts(rand(100))
puts(rand(100))
puts(rand(1))
puts(rand(1))
puts(rand(1))
puts(rand(99999999999999999999999999999999999999))
puts('The weatherman said there is a')
puts(rand(101).to_s + '% chance of rain,')
puts('but you can never trust a weatherman.')
```

Why all the parentheses? Well, when I have several levels of things going on, all on a single line of code, I like to add parentheses to make sure the computer and I agree on just what is supposed to happen.

```
0.780420251671991
0.27612531216364
0.0633567492235
21
12
```

```
99
0
0
0
375328950061142093762388258389027468
The weatherman said there is a
67% chance of rain,
but you can never trust a weatherman.
```

Note that for the weatherman example I used rand(101) to get numbers from 0 to 100 and that rand(1) always returns 0. Not understanding the range of possible return values is the biggest mistake I see people make with rand, even professional programmers, and even in finished products you can buy at the store. I once had a CD player that if set on Random Play, would play every song but the last one. (I wonder what would have happened if I had put in a CD with only one song on it.)

Sometimes you might want rand to return the *same* random numbers in the same sequence on two different runs of your program. (For example, I used randomly generated numbers to generate the worlds in Civilization III. If I found a world that I really liked, I'd save it, run tests on it, and so on.) In order to do this, you need to set the *seed*, which you can do with srand:

```
srand 1976
puts(rand(100))
puts(rand(100))
puts(rand(100))
puts(rand(100))
puts ''
srand 1976
puts(rand(100))
puts(rand(100))
puts(rand(100))
puts(rand(100))
```

```
6
96
69
76

6
96
69
76
```

It will do the same thing every time you seed it with the same number. If you want to get different numbers again (like what happens if you never use srand), then just call srand, passing in no parameter. This seeds it with a really weird number, using (among other things) the current time on your computer, down to the millisecond.

6.6 The Math Object

Finally, let's look at the Math object. They say a code example is worth 1,000 words:

```
puts(Math::PI)
puts(Math::E)
puts(Math.cos(Math::PI/3))
puts(Math.tan(Math::PI/4))
puts(Math.log(Math::E**2))
puts((1 + Math.sqrt(5))/2)
```

```
3.14159265358979
2.71828182845904
0.5
1.0
2.0
1.61803398874989
```

Math::PI is actually *not* a variable; it's a constant. It doesn't vary. Remember how I said that variables in Ruby have to start with a lowercase letter? Constants start with an uppercase letter. The main difference is that Ruby complains if you try to reassign a constant.

The first thing you noticed was probably the :: notation. Explaining the *scope operator* (which is what that is) is beyond the...uh...scope of this book. No pun intended. I swear. Suffice it to say, you can use Math::PI like it were any other variable.

As you can see, Math has all the features you would expect a decent scientific calculator to have. And, as always, the floats are *really close* to being the right answers but not exact; don't trust them further than you can calculate them.

## CHAPTER 7

Flow Control

We've covered a lot of the basics, but this is where we really breathe life into our programs. Up to this point, our programs have been so flat and predictable. Each time we run them, we'll get pretty much the same experience. I mean, if a program asks me for my name, I guess instead of "Chris," I could say "Stud-chunks McStallion" (as they used to call me), but that's hardly a new experience.

After this chapter, though, we'll be able to write truly interactive programs. In the past, we made programs that *said* different things depending on your keyboard input, but after this chapter they will actually *do* different things. But how will we determine when to do one thing instead of another? We need...

7.1 Comparison Methods

You're getting good at this, so I'll try to let the code do the talking. First, to see whether one object is greater than or less than another, we use the methods > and <:

```
puts 1 > 2
puts 1 < 2
```

```
false
true
```

No problem.

Likewise, we can find out whether an object is greater than or equal to another (or less than or equal to) with the methods >= and <=:

```
puts 5 >= 5
puts 5 <= 4
```

```
true
false
```

And finally, we can see whether two objects are equal using == (which means "Are these equal?") and != (which means "Are these different?"). It's important not to confuse = with ==. = is for telling a variable to point at an object (assignment), and == is for asking the question "Are these two objects equal?"

But don't feel too bad if you *do* confuse = and == in your code; I still do it from time to time. Just try to be aware of it.

```
puts 1 == 1
puts 2 != 1
```

```
true
true
```

Of course, we can compare strings, too. When strings get compared, Ruby compares their *lexicographical ordering*, which basically means the order they appear in a dictionary. For example, cat comes before dog in the dictionary, so we have this:

```
puts 'cat' < 'dog'
```

```
true
```

This has a catch, though. The way computers usually do things, they order capital letters as coming before lowercase letters. (That's how they store the letters in fonts—for example, all the capital letters first and then the lowercase ones.) This means it will think 'Xander' comes before 'bug lady'. So if you want to figure out which word would come first in a real dictionary, make sure to use downcase (or upcase or capitalize) on both words before you try to compare them.

```
puts 'bug lady'          < 'Xander'
puts 'bug lady'.downcase < 'Xander'.downcase
```

```
false
true
```

Similarly surprising is this:

```
puts  2  <  10
puts '2' < '10'
```

```
true
false
```

OK, 2 is less than 10, so no problem. But that last one?! Well, the '1' character comes before the '2' character—remember, in a string those are just characters. The '0' character after the '1' doesn't make the '1' any larger.

One last note before we move on: the comparison methods aren't giving us the strings 'true' and 'false'; they are giving us the special objects true and false that represent...well, truth and falsity. (Of course, true.to_s gives us the string 'true', which is why puts printed true.) true and false are used all the time in a language construct called *branching*.

7.2 Branching

Branching is a simple concept, but it's powerful. In fact, it's so simple that I bet I don't even have to explain it at all; I'll just show you:

```
puts 'Hello, what\'s your name?'
name = gets.chomp
puts 'Hello, ' + name + '.'

if name == 'Chris'
  puts 'What a lovely name!'
end
```

```
‹ Hello, what's your name?
⇒ Chris
‹ Hello, Chris.
  What a lovely name!
```

But if we put in a different name...

```
‹ Hello, what's your name?
⇒ Chewbacca
‹ Hello, Chewbacca.
```

And that is branching. If what comes after the if is true, we run the code between the if and the end. If what comes after the if is false, we don't. Plain and simple.

I indented the code between the if and the end just because I think it's easier to keep track of the branching that way. Almost all programmers do this, regardless of what language they are programming in. It may not seem that helpful in this simple example, but when programs get more complex, it makes a big difference. Often, when people send me programs that don't work but they can't figure out why, it's something that is both:

- obvious to see what the problem is if the indentation is nice, and

- impossible to see what the problem is otherwise.

So, try to keep your indentation nice and consistent. Have your if and end line up vertically, and have everything between them indented. I use an indentation of two spaces.

Often, we would like a program to do one thing if an expression is true and another if it is false. That's what else is for.

```
puts 'I am a fortune-teller.  Tell me your name:'
name = gets.chomp

if name == 'Chris'
  puts 'I see great things in your future.'
else
  puts 'Your future is...oh my!  Look at the time!'
  puts 'I really have to go, sorry!'
end
```

```
‹ I am a fortune-teller.  Tell me your name:
⇒ Chris
‹ I see great things in your future.
```

Now let's try a different name:

```
‹ I am a fortune-teller.  Tell me your name:
⇒ Boromir
‹ Your future is...oh my!  Look at the time!
  I really have to go, sorry!
```

And one more:

```
‹ I am a fortune-teller.  Tell me your name:
⇒ Ringo
‹ Your future is...oh my!  Look at the time!
  I really have to go, sorry!
```

Branching is kind of like coming to a fork in the code: do we take the path for people whose name == 'Chris', or else do we take the other, less fortuitous, path? (Well, I guess you could also call it the path of fame, fortune, and glory. But it's my fortune-teller, and I say it's less fortuitous. So there.) Clearly, branching can get pretty deep.

Just like the branches of a tree, you can have branches that themselves have branches, as we can see on the next page.

```
puts 'Hello, and welcome to seventh grade English.'
puts 'My name is Mrs. Gabbard.  And your name is....?'
name = gets.chomp

if name == name.capitalize
  puts 'Please take a seat, ' + name + '.'
else
  puts name + '?  You mean ' + name.capitalize + ', right?'
  puts 'Don\'t you even know how to spell your name??'
  reply = gets.chomp

  if reply.downcase == 'yes'
    puts 'Hmmph!  Well, sit down!'
```

```
    else
       puts 'GET OUT!!'
    end
  end
```

```
‹ Hello, and welcome to seventh grade English.
  My name is Mrs. Gabbard.  And your name is....?
⇒ chris
‹ chris?  You mean Chris, right?
  Don't you even know how to spell your name??
⇒ yes
‹ Hmmph!  Well, sit down!
```

Fine, I'll capitalize my name:

```
‹ Hello, and welcome to seventh grade English.
  My name is Mrs. Gabbard.  And your name is....?
⇒ Chris
‹ Please take a seat, Chris.
```

Sometimes it might get confusing trying to figure out where all the ifs, elses, and ends go. What I do is write the end *at the same time* I write the if. So, as I was writing the previous program, this is how it looked first:

```
puts 'Hello, and welcome to seventh grade English.'
puts 'My name is Mrs. Gabbard.  And your name is....?'
name = gets.chomp

if name == name.capitalize
else
end
```

Then I filled it in with *comments*, stuff in the code the computer will ignore:

```
puts 'Hello, and welcome to seventh grade English.'
puts 'My name is Mrs. Gabbard.  And your name is....?'
name = gets.chomp

if name == name.capitalize
  #  She's civil.
else
  #  She gets mad.
end
```

Anything after a # is considered a comment (unless, of course, the # is in a string). After that, I replaced the comments with working code. Some people like to leave the comments in; personally, I think well-written code usually speaks for itself. (The trick, of course, is in writing well-written code.) I used to use more comments, but the more "fluent" in Ruby I become, the less I use them. I actually find them distracting much of the time. It's a personal choice; you'll find your own (usually evolving) style.

Anyway, my next step looked like this:

```
puts 'Hello, and welcome to seventh grade English.'
puts 'My name is Mrs. Gabbard.  And your name is....?'
name = gets.chomp

if name == name.capitalize
  puts 'Please take a seat, ' + name + '.'
else
  puts name + '?  You mean ' + name.capitalize + ', right?'
  puts 'Don\'t you even know how to spell your name??'
  reply = gets.chomp
  if reply.downcase == 'yes'
  else
  end
end
```

Again, I wrote the if, else, and end all at the same time. It really helps me keep track of "where I am" in the code. It also makes the job seem easier because I can focus on one small part, such as filling in the code between the if and the else. The other benefit of doing it this way is that the computer can understand the program at any stage. Every one of the unfinished versions of the program I showed you would run. They weren't finished, but they were working programs. That way I could test them as I wrote them, which helped me see how my program was coming along and where it still needed work. When it passed all the tests, I knew I was done.

I *strongly* suggest you approach your programs in this way. These tips will help you write programs with branching, but they also help with the other main type of flow control.

7.3 Looping

Often, you'll want your computer to do the same thing over and over again. After all, that's what they're supposed to be good at doing.

When you tell your computer to keep repeating something, you also need to tell it when to stop. Computers never get bored, so if you don't tell it when to stop, it won't.

We make sure this doesn't happen by telling the computer to repeat certain parts of a program while a certain condition is true. It works the way if works:

```
input = ''
while input != 'bye'
  puts input
  input = gets.chomp
end
puts 'Come again soon!'
```

```
<
⇒ Hello?
< Hello?
⇒ Hi!
< Hi!
⇒ Very nice to meet you.
< Very nice to meet you.
⇒ Oh...how sweet!
< Oh...how sweet!
⇒ bye
< Come again soon!
```

It's not a fabulous program, though. For one thing, while tests your condition at the top of the loop. In this case we had to tweak our loop so it could test there. This made us puts a blank line before we did our first gets. In my mind, it just *feels* like the gets comes first and the echoing puts comes later. It'd be nice if we could say something like this:

```
#  THIS IS NOT A REAL PROGRAM!
while just_like_go_forever
  input = gets.chomp
  puts input
  if input == 'bye'
    stop_looping
  end
end

puts 'Come again soon!'
```

That's not valid Ruby code, but it's close! To get it to loop forever, we just need to give while a condition that's always true. And Ruby does have a way to break out of a loop:

```
#  THIS IS SO TOTALLY A REAL PROGRAM!
while 'Spike' > 'Angel'
  input = gets.chomp
  puts input
  if input == 'bye'
    break
  end
end

puts 'Come again soon!'
```

```
⇒ Hi, and your name is...
< Hi, and your name is...
⇒ Cute.  And original.
< Cute.  And original.
⇒ What, are you like... my little brother?!
< What, are you like... my little brother?!
⇒ bye
```

‹ bye
Come again soon!

Now, isn't that better? OK, I'll admit, the 'Spike' > 'Angel' thing is a little silly. When I get bored coming up with jokes for these examples, I'll usually just use the actual true object:

```ruby
while true
  input = gets.chomp
  puts input
  if input == 'bye'
    break
  end
end

puts 'Come again soon!'
```

⇒ **Hey.**
‹ Hey.
⇒ **You again?!**
‹ You again?!
⇒ **bye**
‹ bye
Come again soon!

And that's a loop. It's considerably trickier than a branch, so take a minute to look it over and let it sink in....

Loops are lovely things. However, like high-maintenance girlfriends or bubble gum, they can cause big problems if handled improperly. Here's a big one: what if your computer gets trapped in an infinite loop? If you think this may have happened, just go to your command line, hold down the `Ctrl` key, and press `C`. (You are running these from the command line, right?)

Before we start playing around with loops, though, let's learn a few things to make our job easier.

7.4 A Little Bit of Logic

Mind you, Katy is as lovely and sweet as she is likely to read this book, so I feel I should point out that she would *never* flip out about something like this. She saves that for when I've done something really horrible, like lose one of her James Bond DVDs.

Let's take another look at our first branching program, on page 39. What if my wife came home, saw the program, tried it, and it didn't tell her what a lovely name *she* had? I wouldn't want her to flip out, so let's rewrite it:

```ruby
puts 'Hello, what\'s your name?'
name = gets.chomp
puts 'Hello, ' + name + '.'

if name == 'Chris'
  puts 'What a lovely name!'
else
  if name == 'Katy'
```

```
      puts 'What a lovely name!'
    end
  end
```

⟨ Hello, what's your name?
⇒ **Katy**
⟨ Hello, Katy.
  What a lovely name!

Well, it works…but it isn't a very pretty program. Why not? It just doesn't feel right to me that the whole "Katy" chunk of code is not lined up with the "Chris" chunk of code. These are supposed to be totally equal and symmetrical options, yet one feels distinctly subordinate to the other. (In fact, this code would probably get me sleeping on the couch faster than just leaving her out of the program altogether.) This code just isn't jiving with my mental model.

Fortunately, another Ruby construct can help: elsif. This code means the same thing as the last program but feels so much lovelier:

```
puts 'Hello, what\'s your name?'
name = gets.chomp
puts 'Hello, ' + name + '.'

if    name == 'Chris'
  puts 'What a lovely name!'
elsif name == 'Katy'
  puts 'What a lovely name!'
end
```

⟨ Hello, what's your name?
⇒ **Katy**
⟨ Hello, Katy.
  What a lovely name!

This is a definite improvement, but something is still wrong. If I want the program to do the same thing when it gets *Chris* or *Katy*, then it should really *do the same thing*, as in execute the same code. Here we have two different lines of code doing the same thing. That's not right. That's not how I'm thinking about this.

More pragmatically, it's just a bad idea to duplicate code anywhere. Remember the DRY rule? Don't Repeat Yourself! For pragmatic reasons, for aesthetic reasons, or just because you're lazy, don't *ever* repeat yourself! Weed out duplication in code (or even design) whenever you see it. In our case, we repeated the line puts 'What a lovely name!'. What we're trying to say is just, "If the name is *Chris* or *Katy*, do this." Let's just *code* it that way:

```
puts 'Hello, what\'s your name?'
name = gets.chomp
puts 'Hello, ' + name + '.'

if name == 'Chris' || name == 'Katy'
  puts 'What a lovely name!'
end
```

```
‹ Hello, what's your name?
⇒ Katy
‹ Hello, Katy.
  What a lovely name!
```

Nice. Much, much better. And it's even shorter! I don't know about you, but I'm excited. It's almost the same as the original program! Bliss, I tell you…sparkly programming bliss!

To make it work, I used ||, which is how we say "or" in most programming languages.

At this point, you might be wondering why we couldn't just say this:

```
...
if name == ('Chris' || 'Katy')
  puts 'What a lovely name!'
end
```

It makes sense in English, but you have to remember how staggeringly brilliant humans are compared to computers. The reason this makes sense in English is that humans are just fabulous at dealing with context. In this context, it's clear to a human that "if your name is Chris or Katy" means "if your name is Chris or if it is Katy." (I even used "it"—another triumph of human context handling.) But when your computer sees ('Chris' || 'Katy'), it's not even looking at the name == code; before it gets there, it just tries to figure out whether one of 'Chris' or 'Katy' is true…because that's what || does. But that doesn't really make sense, so you have to be explicit and write the whole thing.

Anyway, that's "or." The other *logical operators* are && ("and") and ! ("not"). Let's see how they work:

```
i_am_chris  = true
i_am_purple = false
i_like_beer = true
i_eat_rocks = false

puts i_am_chris  && i_like_beer
puts i_like_beer && i_eat_rocks
puts i_am_purple && i_like_beer
puts i_am_purple && i_eat_rocks
puts
```

```
puts i_am_chris  || i_like_beer
puts i_like_beer || i_eat_rocks
puts i_am_purple || i_like_beer
puts i_am_purple || i_eat_rocks
puts
puts !i_am_purple
puts !i_am_chris
```

```
true
false
false
false

true
true
true
false

true
false
```

The only one of these that might trick you is ||. In English, we often use "or" to mean "one or the other, but not both." For example, your mom might say, "For dessert, you can have pie or cake." She did *not* mean you could have them both! A computer, on the other hand, uses || to mean "one or the other, or both." (Another way of saying it is "at least one of these is true.") This is why computers are more fun than moms. (Obviously I think my mom is far less likely to read this book than my wife is.)

Just to make sure everything is well cemented for you, let's look at one more example before you go it alone. This will be a simulation of talking to my son, C, back when he was 2. (Just for background, when he talks about Ruby, Nono, and Emma, he is referring to his baby sister, Ruby, and his friends Giuliano and Emma. He manages to bring everyone he loves into every conversation he has. And yes, we did name our children after programming languages. And yes, my wife is the coolest woman ever.) So, without further ado, this is pretty much what happens whenever you ask C to do something:

```
while true
  puts 'What would you like to ask C to do?'
  request = gets.chomp

  puts 'You say, "C, please ' + request + '"'

  puts 'C\'s response:'
  puts '"C '    + request + '."'
  puts '"Papa ' + request + ', too."'
  puts '"Mama ' + request + ', too."'
  puts '"Ruby ' + request + ', too."'
```

```
  puts '"Nono ' + request + ', too."'
  puts '"Emma ' + request + ', too."'
  puts

  if request == 'stop'
    break
  end
end
end
```

Let's chat with C a bit on the next page.

```
‹ What would you like to ask C to do?
⇒ eat
‹ You say, "C, please eat"
  C's response:
  "C eat."
  "Papa eat, too."
  "Mama eat, too."
  "Ruby eat, too."
  "Nono eat, too."
  "Emma eat, too."

  What would you like to ask C to do?
⇒ go potty
‹ You say, "C, please go potty"
  C's response:
  "C go potty."
  "Papa go potty, too."
  "Mama go potty, too."
  "Ruby go potty, too."
  "Nono go potty, too."
  "Emma go potty, too."

  What would you like to ask C to do?
⇒ hush
‹ You say, "C, please hush"
  C's response:
  "C hush."
  "Papa hush, too."
  "Mama hush, too."
  "Ruby hush, too."
  "Nono hush, too."
  "Emma hush, too."

  What would you like to ask C to do?
⇒ stop
‹ You say, "C, please stop"
  C's response:
  "C stop."
  "Papa stop, too."
  "Mama stop, too."
```

```
"Ruby stop, too."
"Nono stop, too."
"Emma stop, too."
```

Yeah, that's about what it was like. You couldn't sneeze without hearing about Emma or Nono sneezing, too.

7.5 A Few Things to Try

- *"99 Bottles of Beer on the Wall."* Write a program that prints out the lyrics to that beloved classic, "99 Bottles of Beer on the Wall."

- *Deaf grandma.* Whatever you say to Grandma (whatever you type in), she should respond with this:

```
HUH?!  SPEAK UP, SONNY!
```

unless you shout it (type in all capitals). If you shout, she can hear you (or at least she thinks so) and yells back:

```
NO, NOT SINCE 1938!
```

To make your program *really* believable, have Grandma shout a different year each time, maybe any year at random between 1930 and 1950. (This part is optional and would be much easier if you read the section on Ruby's random number generator on page 33.) You can't stop talking to Grandma until you shout *BYE*.

Hint 1: Don't forget about chomp! 'BYE' with an Enter at the end is not the same as 'BYE' without one!

Hint 2: Try to think about what parts of your program should happen over and over again. All of those should be in your while loop.

Hint 3: People often ask me, "How can I make rand give me a number in a range not starting at zero?" Well, you can't; rand just doesn't work that way. So, I guess you'll have to do something to the number rand returns to you.

- *Deaf grandma extended.* What if Grandma doesn't want you to leave? When you shout *BYE*, she could pretend not to hear you. Change your previous program so that you have to shout *BYE* three times *in a row*. Make sure to test your program: if you shout *BYE* three times but not in a row, you should still be talking to Grandma.

- *Leap years.* Write a program that asks for a starting year and an ending year and then puts all the leap years between them (and including them, if they are also leap years). Leap years are years divisible by 4 (like 1984 and 2004). However, years divisible by 100 are *not* leap years (such as 1800 and 1900) unless they are also divisible by 400 (such as 1600 and 2000, which were in fact leap years). What a mess!

When you finish those, take a break! That was a *lot* of programming. Congratulations! You're well on your way. Relax, have a nice cold (possibly root) beer, and continue tomorrow.

## CHAPTER 8

Arrays and Iterators

Welcome back! Let's write a program that asks us to type in as many words as we want (one word per line, continuing until we just press Enter on an empty line) and then repeats the words back to us in alphabetical order. OK?

So...first we'll—uh...um...hmmm.... Well, we could—er...em....

You know, I don't think we can do it. We need a way to store an unknown number of words and to keep track of them altogether so they don't get mixed up with other variables. We need to put them in some sort of a list. We need *arrays*.

An array is just a list in your computer. Every slot in the list acts like a variable: you can see what object a particular slot points to, and you can make it point to a different object. Let's take a look at some arrays:

```
[]
[5]
['Hello', 'Goodbye']

flavor = 'vanilla'           #  Not an array, of course...
[89.9, flavor, [true, false]]  #  ...but this is.
```

First we have an empty array, then an array holding a single number, and then an array holding two strings. Next we have a simple assignment; then we have an array holding three objects, the last of which is the array [true, false]. Remember, variables aren't objects, so our last array is really pointing to a float, a *string*, and an array. (Even if we were to set flavor to point to something else later in the program, that wouldn't change the array.)

To help us find a particular object in an array, each slot is given an index number. Programmers (and most mathematicians) like to start counting from zero, though, so the first slot in the array is slot zero. Here's how we would reference the objects in an array:

```
names = ['Ada', 'Belle', 'Chris']
puts names
puts
puts names[0]
puts names[1]
puts names[2]
puts names[3]  # This is out of range.
```

```
Ada
Belle
Chris

Ada
Belle
Chris
nil
```

So, we see that puts names prints each name in the array names. Then we use puts names[0] to print out the *first* name in the array and puts names[1] to print the second. I'm sure this seems confusing, but you *do* get used to it. You just have to really start *thinking* that counting begins at zero and stop using words such as *first* and *second*. If you go out to a five-course meal, don't talk about the first course; talk about course zero (and in your head, be thinking course[0]). You have five fingers on your right hand, and their numbers are 0, 1, 2, 3, and 4. My wife and I are jugglers. When we juggle six clubs, we are juggling clubs 0–5. In the next few months, we hope to be able to juggle club 6 (and thus be juggling seven clubs between us). You'll know you have it when you start using the word *zeroth*.

Finally, we tried puts names[3], just to see what would happen. Were you expecting an error? As we've seen in the past, sometimes when you ask your computer a question, it just doesn't make sense (at least to the computer); that's when you get an error. Sometimes, however, you can ask a question, and the answer is *nothing*. What's in slot three? Nothing. What is names[3]? *nil* : Ruby's way of saying "nothing." nil is a special object that means "not any other object."

Now, I said the slots in your arrays act like variables. This means you can assign to them as well. If you just had to guess what that code looked like, you'd probably guess something like this:

Others who were in C's oft-repeated list: baby Edison, Mercedes, and baby Melena.

```
other_peeps = []
other_peeps[3] = 'beebee Meaner'
other_peeps[0] = 'Ah-ha'
other_peeps[1] = 'Seedee'
other_peeps[0] = 'beebee Ah-ha'
puts other_peeps
```

```
beebee Ah-ha
Seedee
nil
beebee Meaner
```

As you can see, you don't have to assign to the slots in any particular order, and any you leave empty are filled with nil by default.

If all this funny numbering of array slots is getting to you, fear not! Often, we can avoid them completely by using various array methods, such as each.

8.1 The Method each

The method each allows us to do something (whatever we want) to *each* object the array points to. (It looks weird, though, and this can throw people off, so brace yourself.)

For example, if we want to say something nice about each language in the following array, we could do something like this:

```
languages = ['English', 'Norwegian', 'Ruby']

languages.each do |lang|
  puts 'I love ' + lang + '!'
  puts 'Don\'t you?'
end

puts 'And let\'s hear it for Java!'
puts '<crickets chirp in the distance>'
```

```
I love English!
Don't you?
I love Norwegian!
Don't you?
I love Ruby!
Don't you?
And let's hear it for Java!
<crickets chirp in the distance>
```

What just happened? (Aside from Java getting pwn3d, heh-heh.) Well, we were able to go through every object in the array without using any numbers, so that's definitely nice. There are those weird vertical-bar-thingies around lang; I'll get to that. But first, just to make sure you understand what this code means (if not necessarily *why* it means it), let's translate it into English: for each object in languages, point the variable lang to the object, and then do everything I tell you to, until you come to the end.

We use do and end to specify a block of code. In this case, we're sending that block to the each method, saying "This is what I want you to do with each of the objects in the array." Blocks are great, but a bit advanced, which is why we're not *really* going to talk about them until Chapter 14, *Blocks and Procs*, on page 113. Until then, however, we can still use them. We just won't talk about them. Much.

Except we'll talk about the vertical-bar-thingies, like in |lang|. It looks weird, but the idea is simple: lang is the variable that each will use to point to the objects in the array. How would we otherwise refer to the string 'English'? (Well, maybe using languages[0], but the whole point here was to avoid messing with the slot numbers.) The vertical bars don't *do* anything to lang; they just let each know which variable to use to feed in the objects in the array.

You might be thinking to yourself, "This is a lot like the loops we learned about earlier." Yep, it's similar. One important difference is that the method each is just that: a method. while and end (much like do, if, else, and all the other keywords) are not methods. They are a fundamental part of the Ruby language, just like = and parentheses; they are kind of like punctuation marks in English.

But this isn't true with each; each is just another array method. Methods like each that "act like" loops are often called *iterators*.

One thing to notice about iterators is that they are always followed by a block—that is, by some code wrapped inside do...end. On the other hand, while and if never had a do near them.

Here's another cute little iterator, but this one is not an array method:

```ruby
# Go-go-gadget-integer-method...
3.times do
  puts 'Hip-Hip-Hooray!'
end
```

```
Hip-Hip-Hooray!
Hip-Hip-Hooray!
Hip-Hip-Hooray!
```

It's an integer method. Now you cannot *tell* me that ain't the cutest code you've ever seen! And, as promised on page 17, here's that pretty program again:

```ruby
2.times do
  puts '...you can say that again...'
end
```

```
...you can say that again...
...you can say that again...
```

8.2 More Array Methods

We've learned each, but there are many other array methods, almost as many as there are string methods. In fact, some of them (such as length, reverse, +, and *) work just like they do for strings, except they operate on the slots of the array rather than on the letters of the string. Others, such as last and join, are specific to arrays. Still others, such as push and pop, actually change the array. And just as with the string methods, you don't have to remember all of these, as long as you can remember where to find out about them (and that would be right here).

Let's look at to_s and join. join works much like to_s does, except that it adds a string in between the array's objects. Actually, I can't think of a time when I have *ever* used to_s on any array. I always use puts or join. But I know you're dying to know how to_s works, so take a look at the following example:

```
foods = ['artichoke', 'brioche', 'caramel']

puts foods
puts
puts foods.to_s
puts
puts foods.join(', ')
puts
puts foods.join('  :)  ') + '  8)'

200.times do
  puts []
end
```

Two hundred times?! No more sugar for me!

```
artichoke
brioche
caramel

[artichoke, brioche, caramel]

artichoke, brioche, caramel

artichoke :) brioche :) caramel 8)
```

Whew! It's good puts treats arrays differently from other objects; that would have been a boring couple of pages if puts had written something 200 times. With arrays, puts calls puts on each of the objects in the array. That's why calling puts on an empty array 200 times doesn't do anything; the array doesn't contain anything, so there's nothing to puts. Doing nothing 200 times is still doing nothing (unless you're playing a role-playing game, in which case you just leveled!). Try putsing an array containing other arrays; did it do what you expected?

Now let's take a look at push, pop, and last. The methods push and pop are sort of opposites, like + and - are. push adds an object to the end of your array, and pop removes the last object from the array (and tells you what it was). last is similar to pop in that it tells you what's at the end of the array, except that it leaves the array alone. Again, push and pop *actually change the array*:

```
favorites = []
favorites.push 'raindrops on roses'
favorites.push 'whiskey on kittens'

puts favorites[0]
puts favorites.last
puts favorites.length

puts favorites.pop
puts favorites
puts favorites.length
```

```
raindrops on roses
whiskey on kittens
2
whiskey on kittens
raindrops on roses
1
```

8.3   A Few Things to Try

- *Building and sorting an array.* Write the program we talked about at the beginning of this chapter, one that asks us to type as many words as we want (one word per line, continuing until we just press `Enter` on an empty line) and then repeats the words back to us in alphabetical order. Make sure to test your program thoroughly; for example, does hitting `Enter` on an empty line *always* exit your program? Even on the first line? And the second? *Hint:* There's a lovely array method that will give you a sorted version of an array: sort. Use it!

- *Table of contents, revisited.* Rewrite your table of contents program on page 32. Start the program with an array holding all of the information for your table of contents (chapter names, page numbers, and so on). Then print out the information from the array in a beautifully formatted table of contents.

## CHAPTER 9

Writing Your Own Methods

As we've seen, loops and iterators allow us to do the same thing (run the same code) over and over again. However, sometimes we want to do the same thing a number of times but from different places in the program. For example, let's say we were writing a questionnaire program for a psychology student. From the psychology students I have known and the questionnaires they have given me, it would probably go something like this:

```ruby
puts 'Hello, and thank you for taking the time to'
puts 'help me with this experiment.  My experiment'
puts 'has to do with the way people feel about'
puts 'Mexican food.  Just think about Mexican food'
puts 'and try to answer every question honestly,'
puts 'with either a "yes" or a "no".  My experiment'
puts 'has nothing to do with bed-wetting.'
puts
#  We ask these questions, but we ignore their answers.
while true
  puts 'Do you like eating tacos?'
  answer = gets.chomp.downcase
  if (answer == 'yes' || answer == 'no')
    break
  else
    puts 'Please answer "yes" or "no".'
  end
end

while true
  puts 'Do you like eating burritos?'
  answer = gets.chomp.downcase
  if (answer == 'yes' || answer == 'no')
    break
  else
    puts 'Please answer "yes" or "no".'
  end
end
```

```ruby
#  We pay attention to *this* answer, though.
while true
  puts 'Do you wet the bed?'
  answer = gets.chomp.downcase
  if (answer == 'yes' || answer == 'no')
    if answer == 'yes'
      wets_bed = true
    else
      wets_bed = false
    end
    break
  else
    puts 'Please answer "yes" or "no".'
  end
end

while true
  puts 'Do you like eating chimichangas?'
  answer = gets.chomp.downcase
  if (answer == 'yes' || answer == 'no')
    break
  else
    puts 'Please answer "yes" or "no".'
  end
end

puts 'Just a few more questions...'

while true
  puts 'Do you like eating sopapillas?'
  answer = gets.chomp.downcase
  if (answer == 'yes' || answer == 'no')
    break
  else
    puts 'Please answer "yes" or "no".'
  end
end

#  Ask lots of other questions about Mexican food.

puts
puts 'DEBRIEFING:'
puts 'Thank you for taking the time to help with'
puts 'this experiment.  In fact, this experiment'
puts 'has nothing to do with Mexican food.  It is'
puts 'an experiment about bed-wetting.  The Mexican'
puts 'food was just there to catch you off guard'
puts 'in the hopes that you would answer more'
puts 'honestly.  Thanks again.'
puts
puts wets_bed
```

```
‹ Hello, and thank you for taking the time to
  help me with this experiment. My experiment
  has to do with the way people feel about
  Mexican food. Just think about Mexican food
  and try to answer every question honestly,
  with either a "yes" or a "no". My experiment
  has nothing to do with bed-wetting.

  Do you like eating tacos?
⇒ yes
‹ Do you like eating burritos?
⇒ yes
‹ Do you wet the bed?
⇒ no way!
‹ Please answer "yes" or "no".
  Do you wet the bed?
⇒ NO
‹ Do you like eating chimichangas?
⇒ yes
```

```
‹ Just a few more questions...
  Do you like eating sopapillas?
⇒ yes
‹
  DEBRIEFING:
  Thank you for taking the time to help with
  this experiment. In fact, this experiment
  has nothing to do with Mexican food. It is
  an experiment about bed-wetting. The Mexican
  food was just there to catch you off guard
  in the hopes that you would answer more
  honestly. Thanks again.

  false
```

Psych majors.... Anyway, that was a pretty long program—a long, ugly program with lots of ugly repetition. All of the sections of code around the questions about Mexican food were identical except for the food, and the bed-wetting question was only slightly different.

As we've talked about before, repetition is a Bad Thing. Still, we can't change the repeated code to a big loop or iterator, because sometimes we have things we want to do between questions. In situations like these, it's best to write a method of your own. Let's start with something small and return to the psych program later.

Let's write a method that just says "moo":

```
def say_moo
  puts 'mooooooo...'
end
```

Um...our program didn't say_moo. Why not? Because we didn't tell it to. We told it *how* to say_moo, but we never actually said to *do* it. Let's give it another shot.

```
def say_moo
  puts 'mooooooo...'
end

say_moo
say_moo
puts 'coin-coin'
say_moo
say_moo
```

```
mooooooo...
mooooooo...
coin-coin
mooooooo...
mooooooo...
```

Ahhh, much better.

Just in case you don't speak French, that was a French duck in the middle of the program. The ducks over there say "coin-coin," I hear. Unfortunately, the only things I retained from Compulsory French 101 were that and a few words I'm not allowed to write (in case we ever decide to translate this book into Canadian).

So, we defined the method say_moo. (Method names, like variable names, almost always start with a lowercase letter. There are a few exceptions, though, such as + or ==.) But don't methods always have to be associated with objects? Well, yes, they do, and in this case (as with puts and gets), the method is just associated with the object representing the whole program. In Chapter 13, *Creating New Classes, Changing Existing Ones*, on page 103, we'll see how to add methods to other objects. But first...

9.1 Method Parameters

You may have noticed that some methods (such as gets, reverse, to_s, and so on) can just be called on an object. However, other methods (such as +, -, puts...) take *parameters* to tell the object how to do the method. For example, you wouldn't just say 5+, right? You're telling 5 to add, but you aren't telling it *what* to add.

To add a parameter to say_moo (let's say, the number of moos), we would do the following:

```
def say_moo number_of_moos
  puts 'mooooooo...'*number_of_moos
end

say_moo 3
puts 'oink-oink'

#  This last line should give an error
#  because the parameter is missing...
say_moo
```

```
mooooooo...mooooooo...mooooooo...
oink-oink
#<ArgumentError: wrong number of arguments (0 for 1)>
```

number_of_moos is a variable that points to the parameter passed in. I'll say that again, but it's a little confusing: number_of_moos is a variable that points to the parameter passed in. So, if I type say_moo 3, then the parameter is 3, and the variable number_of_moos points to 3.

As you can see, the parameter is now *required*. After all, what is say_moo supposed to multiply 'mooooooo...' by if you don't give it a parameter? Your poor computer has no idea.

If objects in Ruby are like nouns in English and methods are like verbs, then you can think of parameters as adverbs (like with say_moo, where the parameter told us *how* to say_moo) or sometimes as direct objects (like with puts, where the parameter is *what* gets putsed).

9.2 Local Variables

The following program has two variables:

```
def double_this num
  num_times_2 = num*2
  puts num.to_s+' doubled is '+num_times_2.to_s
end

double_this 44
```

```
44 doubled is 88
```

The variables are num and num_times_2. They both sit inside the method double_this. These (and all the variables you have seen so far) are *local variables*. This means they live inside the method, and they cannot leave. If you try, you will get an error:

```
def double_this num
  num_times_2 = num*2
  puts num.to_s+' doubled is '+num_times_2.to_s
end
double_this 44
puts num_times_2.to_s
```

```
44 doubled is 88
#<NameError: undefined local variable 'num_times_2'>
```

Undefined local variable…. In fact, we *did* define that local variable, but it isn't local to where we tried to use it; it's local to the method, which means it's local to double_this.

This might seem inconvenient, but it's actually quite nice. Although it does mean you have no access to variables inside methods, it also means they have no access to *your* variables and thus can't screw them up, as the following example shows:

```
tough_var = 'You can\'t even touch my variable!'

def little_pest tough_var
  tough_var = nil
  puts 'HAHA!  I ruined your variable!'
end

little_pest tough_var
puts tough_var
```

```
HAHA!  I ruined your variable!
You can't even touch my variable!
```

In fact, *two* variables in that little program are named tough_var: one inside little_pest and one outside of it. They don't communicate. They aren't related. They aren't even friends. When we called little_pest tough_var, we really just passed the string from one tough_var to the other (via the method call, the only way they can even sort of communicate) so that both were pointing to the same string. Then little_pest pointed its own *local* tough_var to nil, but that did nothing to the tough_var variable outside the method.

9.3 Experiment: Duby

OK, local variables, neat trick…but maybe you're wondering, "What's the point?" Legitimate question, but it's kind of hard to see the point without considering what it would be like *without* local variables. It's like if you'd never seen a seatbelt, and I'm here telling you all about the different tension mechanisms, how it connects to the car, and the different kinds of latches, and you're all, "And the point is…?" Well, imagine a world without seatbelts. You get in a wreck. You fly out the window. You die.

The negative consequences of programming without local variables are certainly not as dramatic, but neither are they as easily explained. To get a feel for life without locals, let's imagine a fake language called Duby (for *Dumb Ruby*).

Duby is just like regular Ruby, except that all variables live in the same scope (that is, they have the same visibility). There's no idea of local or global. Let's say we wanted to make a method to square a number:

```
def square x
  puts(x * x)
end
```

Now we've used the variable x here, but we're just using it as a placeholder. What I mean is, we could just as well have used y or my_fabulous_number; it should make no difference, right? The whole point is to say that the square of *something* is just "something times something." That's the abstraction that methods provide. In this particular case, no matter what variable you are squaring, "the square of something" simply means "something times something." That's what you're trying to say when you define this method.

Now let's say, in Duby, you wrote this:

```
x = 5
square x
```

Now at this point, assuming you defined square like we did earlier, then x is pointing to 5, before and after we called square. No problem.

And what about this program (again, in Duby)?

```
my_number = 5
square my_number
```

Basically it's the same program, just with a different variable name. Now my_number is pointing to 5. But what about x? What is it pointing to?

I guess it would also have to be 5. In order to use the square method, the value passed into it (5, pointed to by my_number) needs to be assigned to x (that is, have x point to it) before you can run the x * x code. So, x is 5. So far, so good.

Now consider this code:

```
x = 10
my_number = x / 2
square my_number
```

In this case, my_number is half of x (so it must be 5), but that means x must also have been set to 5 when we called square, even though we had just set it to 10.

And this is the big bad: calling the square method displays the squared value, but it *also* has the nasty side effect of resetting x to be whatever was passed in. This is Just Plain Wrong. I mean, x used to be 10! Now it's 5! This is insane.

What if we don't *want* any of our variables to be changed? What if we just want to display the square of whatever number we pass in? Can we get around the problem of the unintended side effects? Maybe.

We could start defining all of our methods like this:

```
def square liauwechygfakcuewhalcufe
  liauwechygfakcuewhalcufe * liauwechygfakcuewhalcufe
end
```

And we could just hope that we don't use liauwechygfakcuewhalcufe anywhere else in the program, but that hardly seems ideal. I'm not going to write code like that, and neither should you. Can't we do better than this?

What if the x used in the square method was a *different* x, a totally private x that we use only for the square method; it doesn't mean "the x you were using." It's just a temporary name for this value. It's just a *local* variable.

That's exactly what Ruby does. (And just about every other programming language.)

9.4 Return Values

You may have noticed that some methods give you something back when you call them. For example, we say gets *returns* a string (the string you typed in), and the + method in 5+3 (which is really 5.+(3)) returns 8. The arithmetic methods for numbers return numbers, and the arithmetic methods for strings return strings.

It's important to understand the difference between a method returning a value (returning it to the code that called the method), and your program outputting information to your screen, like puts does. Notice that 5+3 returns 8; it does *not* output 8 (that is, display 8 on your screen).

So, what *does* puts return? We never cared before, but let's look at it now:

```
return_val = puts 'This puts returned:'
puts return_val
```

```
This puts returned:
nil
```

The first puts returned nil. Though we didn't test it, the second puts did, too; puts always returns nil. Every method has to return something, even if it's just nil.

Take a quick break, and write a program to find out what say_moo returns.

Are you surprised? Well, here's how it works: the value returned from a method is simply the last *expression* evaluated in the method (usually just the last line of the method). In the case of say_moo, this means it returns puts 'mooooooo...' *number_of_moos, which is just nil since puts always returns nil. If we wanted all our methods to return the string 'yellow submarine', we would just need to put *that* at the end of them:

```
def say_moo number_of_moos
  puts 'mooooooo...'*number_of_moos
  'yellow submarine'
end

x = say_moo 3
puts x.capitalize + ', dude...'
puts x           + '.'
```

```
mooooooo...mooooooo...mooooooo...
Yellow submarine, dude...
yellow submarine.
```

(I have no idea why you'd want say_moo to work that way, but there you have it.)

Notice I said "the last expression evaluated" instead of simply "the last line" or even "the last expression"; it's possible for the last line to be only a small part of an expression (like the end in an if expression), and it's possible for the last expression not to be evaluated at all if the method has an explicit return:

```
def favorite_food name
  if name == 'Lister'
    return 'vindaloo'
  end

  if name == 'Rimmer'
    return 'mashed potatoes'
  end

  'hard to say...maybe fried plantain?'
end

def favorite_drink name
  if name == 'Jean-Luc'
    'tea, Earl Grey, hot'
  elsif name == 'Kathryn'
    'coffee, black'
```

```ruby
    else
      'perhaps...horchata?'
    end
end

puts favorite_food('Rimmer')
puts favorite_food('Lister')
puts favorite_food('Cher')
puts favorite_drink('Kathryn')
puts favorite_drink('Oprah')
puts favorite_drink('Jean-Luc')
```

```
mashed potatoes
vindaloo
hard to say...maybe fried plantain?
coffee, black
perhaps...horchata?
tea, Earl Grey, hot
```

Make sure you follow each of the six delicious examples.

I did two different things in that program: with favorite_food I used explicit re-turns, and in favorite_drink I didn't. Depending on the feel of the code, I'll write a method one way or the other. If I'm trying to prune off special cases, I might use returns and leave the general case on the last line. If I think the options are all of relatively equal importance, I might use elsif and else like that...feels more egalitarian, you know?

I feel like I'm supposed to tell you now that it doesn't make any difference which way you use; it is *just* a matter of style. But I don't believe that. You want your code to reflect your *intent*, not just the solution. You want your code to be beautiful.

OK, now that we can write our own methods, let's try that psychology exper-iment program again. This time we'll write a method to ask the questions for us. It will need to take the question as a parameter and return true if the person answers *yes* and false if they answer *no*. (Even though most of the time we just ignore the answer, it's still a good idea for our method to return the answer. This way we can use it for the bed-wetting question, too.) I'm also going to shorten the greeting and the debriefing, just so this is easier to read:

```ruby
def ask question
  while true
    puts question
    reply = gets.chomp.downcase

    if (reply == 'yes' || reply == 'no')
      if reply == 'yes'
        answer = true
      else
        answer = false
      end
      break
    else
      puts 'Please answer "yes" or "no".'
```

```
      end
    end

    answer  #  This is what we return (true or false).
  end

  puts 'Hello, and thank you for...'
  puts

  ask 'Do you like eating tacos?'         #  Ignore this return value
  ask 'Do you like eating burritos?'      #  And this one
  wets_bed = ask 'Do you wet the bed?'    #  Save this return value
  ask 'Do you like eating chimichangas?'
  ask 'Do you like eating sopapillas?'
  puts 'Just a few more questions...'
  ask 'Do you like drinking horchata?'
  ask 'Do you like eating flautas?'

  puts
  puts 'DEBRIEFING:'
  puts 'Thank you for...'
  puts
  puts wets_bed
```

```
❮ Hello, and thank you for...

  Do you like eating tacos?
⇒ yes
❮ Do you like eating burritos?
⇒ yes
❮ Do you wet the bed?
⇒ no way!
❮ Please answer "yes" or "no".
  Do you wet the bed?
⇒ NO
❮ Do you like eating chimichangas?
⇒ yes
❮ Do you like eating sopapillas?
⇒ yes
❮ Just a few more questions...
  Do you like drinking horchata?
⇒ yes
❮ Do you like eating flautas?
⇒ yes
❮
  DEBRIEFING:
  Thank you for...

  false
```

Not bad, huh? We were able to add more questions (and adding questions is *easy* now), but our program is still quite a bit shorter. Nice...a lazy programmer's dream.

9.5 A Few Things to Try

- *Improved ask method.* That ask method I showed you was OK, but I bet you could do better. Try to clean it up by removing the answer variable. You'll have to use return to exit from the loop. (Well, it will get you out of the whole method, but it will get you out of the loop in the process.) How do you like the resulting method? I usually try to avoid using return (a personal preference), but I might make an exception here.

- *Old-school Roman numerals.* In the early days of Roman numerals, the Romans didn't bother with any of this new-fangled subtraction "IX" nonsense. No sir, it was straight addition, biggest to littlest—so 9 was written "VIIII," and so on. Write a method that when passed an integer between 1 and 3000 (or so) returns a string containing the proper old-school Roman numeral. In other words, old_roman_numeral 4 should return 'IIII'. Make sure to test your method on a bunch of different numbers. *Hint:* Use the integer division and modulus methods on page 32.

  For reference, these are the values of the letters used:

I = 1	V = 5	X = 10	L = 50
C = 100	D = 500	M = 1000	

My bet is that it was a stone carver in some year that ended in a 9, tasked with dating public buildings or statues or something.

- *"Modern" Roman numerals.* Eventually, someone thought it would be terribly clever if putting a smaller number before a larger one meant you had to subtract the smaller one. As a result of this development, you must now suffer. Rewrite your previous method to return the new-style Roman numerals so when someone calls roman_numeral 4, it should return 'IV'.

There's Nothing New to Learn in Chapter 10

Congratulations! You're a programmer! At this point we've covered most of the basics of programming. The rest of the book is pretty much just fleshing things out for you, showing a few tricks, presenting ways to save time, and so on.

But it hasn't been easy, I imagine. If your brain isn't already hurting by this point, either you're brilliant, you were already a programmer before picking up this book, or you do not yet comprehend the power (and terror) of what you've just learned.

Since you've done so well making it this far, I'll make you a deal: we won't cover anything new in this chapter! We'll just sort of...reminisce.

This should make all of our lives a bit easier.

10.1 Recursion

You know how to make methods, and you know how to call methods. (Your very first program did that! Ahhh, those simple days of one-line programs....) When you write methods, you'll usually fill them with method calls. You can make methods, and they can call methods...see where I'm going with this? Yeah? No?

What if you wrote a method that called itself?

That's *recursion*.

Well, on the surface, it's an absurd idea; if all a method did was call itself, which would just call itself again, it would loop like that forever. (Although this is not technically a loop, it is similar; we can usually replace loops with recursion if we feel like it.) But of course, it could do other things as well and maybe call itself only some of the time.

Let's look at what our `ask` method from our psych program would look like with recursion instead of `while` loops:

```ruby
def ask_recursively question
  puts question
  reply = gets.chomp.downcase

  if    reply == 'yes'
    true
  elsif reply == 'no'
    false
  else
    puts 'Please answer "yes" or "no".'
    ask_recursively question  # This is the magic line.
  end
end

ask_recursively 'Do you wet the bed?'
```

```
‹ Do you wet the bed?
⇒ no way!
‹ Please answer "yes" or "no".
  Do you wet the bed?
⇒ NO, dude!
‹ Please answer "yes" or "no".
  Do you wet the bed?
⇒ I said, "NO!"
‹ Please answer "yes" or "no".
  Do you wet the bed?
⇒ NOOOOOOOOOOOOOOOOOOO!!!!!
‹ Please answer "yes" or "no".
  Do you wet the bed?
⇒ nononononononononono
‹ Please answer "yes" or "no".
  Do you wet the bed?
⇒ <gasp>
‹ Please answer "yes" or "no".
  Do you wet the bed?
⇒ yes
```

Oh, *nice!* That is smooth, with a capital *Smooth*...er, as they say. Wow. Now I feel kind of bad about pushing that sorry loop version onto you in the previous chapter. This one is super short, has no unnecessary variables, and has no returns; it just does what it does.

As *who* said? Ten points if you know.

Honestly, I'm a little surprised at how nice that was. I would not normally have thought of using recursion here. In general, I try to use loops when I'm going to be doing the same thing over and over again, and I use recursion when a small part of the problem resembles the whole problem; the classic example is in computing factorials. Maybe I should think about using recursion more often....

Anyway, since I brought them up and since there seems to be some universal law that every introduction to recursion involves computing factorials, we might as well give it a whirl. I'm feeling pretty rebellious, anyway, for not using factorials as my *first* recursion example, so look at this before the recursion police take me away:

```
def factorial num
  if num < 0
    return 'You can\'t take the factorial of a negative number!'
  end

  if num <= 1
    1
  else
    num * factorial(num-1)
  end
end

puts factorial(3)
puts factorial(30)
```

```
6
265252859812191058636308480000000
```

There you are: factorials. For those of you who had better things to do than go to math class (clearly I did not), the factorial of an integer is the product of all the integers from itself down to 1. In other words, the factorial of 3 (written 3!, as if to fool you into thinking factorials are really exciting) is just 3 times 2 times 1, or 6. And 0! is 1 (I could give you a "sound of one hand clapping" sort of argument you may or may not find satisfying, or you could just take my word for it), and the factorial of a negative number is just plain bad sportsmanship.

But these examples have been sort of contrived (though I did end up really liking how ask_recursively turned out). How about a real example?

When I was generating the worlds for the game Civilization III, I wanted worlds with two primary supercontinents; those tend to be a lot of fun and just sort of feel "earthy" and...*real*. So after I generated the land masses (which was some pretty clever programming there, too), I wanted to test them to see what the sizes of the different continents were. If there were two of relatively equal size (say, differing by a factor of 2 or less) and no others close in size, I'd say that was a pretty good world.

The process, then, was something like the following:

1. Build the world.

2. Find a "continent" (which could be a one-tile island...at this point I wouldn't know).

3. Compute its size.

4. Find another continent (making sure not to count any of them twice but also making sure each gets counted), and repeat the process.

5. Then find the largest two, and see whether they look like fun to play on.

The fun part (actually, it was all fun, not just this part!) was in computing each continent's size, because the best way to do that was recursively.

Let's look at a trimmed-down version. Let's say we have an 11x11 world (represented as an array of arrays...basically just a grid) and that we want to find the size of the continent in the middle (that is, the continent of which tile (5,5) is a part). We don't want to count any land tiles belonging to any of the other continents. Also, as in Civilization III, we'll say that tiles touching only at the corners are still considered to be on the same continent (since units could walk along diagonals).

But before we get to the code, let's solve the problem in English first. My initial plan was to look at every tile on the map, and if that tile is a land tile on the continent I'm looking for, we add 1 to the running total. The problem, though, is how do we know whether a land tile is on the same continent as some other land tile? There are ways to solve this problem, but they all seemed to be too messy; either I was keeping track of lots of information I didn't feel like I needed or I seemed to be doing the same computation over and over again.

But then I thought, hey, two tiles are on the same continent if you can walk from one to the other. (That was essentially the operating definition of continent in Civilization III.) So that's how the code should work! First, you count the spot you are standing on (duh); in this case, that means tile (5,5). Then, you send out eight little guys, one in each direction, and tell them to count the rest of the continent in that direction. The only rule is that no one can count a tile that someone else has already counted. When those eight guys return, you add their answers to your already-running total (which is just 1, from the tile you started with), and that's your answer.

Brilliant! Except for one tiny little detail...how are those eight little guys supposed to determine the size of the continent? You just shrugged the problem onto them! The only tile you counted was the one you were standing on. This is pretty frickin' lazy. Which is probably a good thing....

How are your eight little helpers supposed to compute the size of the continent? The same way you do! So somehow, by a bunch of little, lazy, imaginary helpers counting only the tile they are on, you get the size of the whole continent. (We still need to make sure no tile is counted twice, but we can just mark each tile as it is visited to keep track.) Without further ado, behold the magic of recursion.

```ruby
#  These are just to make the map easier for me to read.
#  "M" is visually more dense than "o".
M = 'land'
o = 'water'

world = [[o,o,o,o,o,o,o,o,o,o,o],
         [o,o,o,o,M,M,o,o,o,o,o],
         [o,o,o,o,o,o,o,o,M,M,o],
         [o,o,o,M,o,o,o,o,o,M,o],
         [o,o,o,M,o,M,M,o,o,o,o],
         [o,o,o,o,M,M,M,M,o,o,o],
         [o,o,o,M,M,M,M,M,M,M,o],
         [o,o,o,M,M,o,M,M,M,o,o],
         [o,o,o,o,o,o,M,M,o,o,o],
         [o,M,o,o,o,M,o,o,o,o,o],
         [o,o,o,o,o,o,o,o,o,o,o]]

def continent_size world, x, y
  if world[y][x] != 'land'
    #  Either it's water or we already counted it,
    #  but either way, we don't want to count it now.
    return 0
  end
  #  So first we count this tile...
  size = 1
  world[y][x] = 'counted land'

  #  ...then we count all of the neighboring eight tiles
  #  (and, of course, their neighbors by  way of the recursion).
  size = size + continent_size(world, x-1, y-1)
  size = size + continent_size(world, x  , y-1)
  size = size + continent_size(world, x+1, y-1)
  size = size + continent_size(world, x-1, y  )
  size = size + continent_size(world, x+1, y  )
  size = size + continent_size(world, x-1, y+1)
  size = size + continent_size(world, x  , y+1)
  size = size + continent_size(world, x+1, y+1)
  size
end

puts continent_size(world, 5, 5)
```

Drumroll, please....

```
23
```

And there you have it. Even if the world was much, much larger and the continent was totally bizarre and oddly shaped, it would still work just fine. Well, there is actually one small bug for you to fix. This code works fine because the continent does not border the edge of the world. If it did, then when we send our little guys out (that is, call continent_size on a new tile), some of them would fall off the edge of the world (that is, call continent_size with invalid values for x and/or y), which would probably crash on the very first line of the method.

It seems like the obvious way to fix this would be to do a check before each call to continent_size (sort of like sending your little guys out only if they aren't going to fall over the edge of the world), but that would require eight separate (yet nearly identical) checks in your method. Yuck. It would be lazier to just send your guys out and have them shout back "ZERO!" if they fall off the edge of the world. (In other words, put the check right at the top of the method, very much like the check we put in to see whether the tile was uncounted land.) Go for it! Of course, you'll have to make sure it works; test it by extending the continent to touch one (or better yet, all four) of the edges of the world.

And that, my friends, is recursion. It's not really anything new, just a new way of thinking of the same old stuff you already learned.

10.2 Rite of Passage: Sorting

Remember the sorting program you wrote on page 56 where you asked for a list of words, sorted it, and then displayed the sorted list? The program was made much easier because you used the array's sort method. But, like the Jedi who constructs his own lightsaber, you'll exhibit a greater mastery if you write your own sorting method. Hey, we've all done it. It's not easy, but this kind of problem solving is part of nearly every program you'll write, so you'd best get your practice now.

But where do you begin? Much like with continent_size, it's probably best to try to solve the problem in English first. Then translate it into Ruby when you've wrapped your head around it.

So, we want to sort an array of words, and we know how to find out which of two words comes first in the dictionary (using <).

What strikes me as probably the easiest way to do this is to keep two more lists around: one will be our list of already-sorted words, and the other will be our list of still-unsorted words. We'll take our list of words, find the "smallest" word (that is, the word that would come first in the dictionary), and stick it at the end of the already-sorted list. All of the other words go into the still-unsorted list. Then you do the same thing again but using the still-unsorted list instead of your original list: find the smallest word, move it to the sorted list, and move the rest to the unsorted list. Keep going until your still-unsorted list is empty.

That doesn't sound too bad, but it's keeping all of the details straight that makes it so tricky. Go ahead and try it, and see how it looks. In fact, try it twice: once using recursion and once without. With the recursion, you might need a *wrapper method*, a tiny method that wraps up another method into a cute little package, like this:

```ruby
def sort some_array  # This "wraps" recursive_sort.
  recursive_sort some_array, []
end

def recursive_sort unsorted_array, sorted_array
  # Your fabulous code goes here.
end
```

What was the point of the wrapper method? Well, recursive_sort took two parameters, but if you were just trying to sort an array, you would always have to pass in an empty array as the second parameter. This is a silly thing to have to remember. Here, the wrapper method passes it in for us, so we never have to think about it again.

When you're done, make sure to test your code! Type in duplicate words and things like that. A great way to test would be to use the built-in sort method to get a sorted version of your list right away. Then, after you have sorted it for yourself, make sure the two lists are equal.

10.3 A Few Things to Try

- *Shuffle.* Now that you've finished your new sorting algorithm, how about the opposite? Write a shuffle method that takes an array and returns a totally shuffled version. As always, you'll want to test it, but testing this one is trickier: How can you test to make sure you are getting a perfect shuffle? What would you even say a perfect shuffle would be? Now test for it.

- *Dictionary sort.* Your sorting algorithm is pretty good, sure. But there was always that sort of embarrassing point you were hoping I'd just sort of gloss over, right? About the capital letters? Your sorting algorithm is good for general-purpose sorting, but when you sort strings, you are using the ordering of the characters in your fonts (called the *ASCII codes*) rather than true dictionary ordering. In a dictionary, case (upper or lower) is irrelevant to the ordering. So, make a new method to sort words (something like dictionary_sort). Remember, though, that if I give your program words starting with capital letters, it should return words with those same capital letters, just ordered as you'd find in a dictionary.

10.4 One More Example

I think another example method would be helpful here. We'll call this one english_number. It will take a number, like 22, and return the English version of it (in this case, the string 'twenty-two'). For now, let's have it work only on integers from 0 to 100:

```ruby
def english_number number
  # We accept numbers from 0 to 100.
  if number < 0
    return 'Please enter a number zero or greater.'
  end
  if number > 100
    return 'Please enter a number 100 or less.'
  end

  num_string = ''  # This is the string we will return.

  # "left"  is how much of the number
  #         we still have left to write out.
  # "write" is the part we are
  #         writing out right now.
  # write and left... get it?  :)
  left  = number
  write = left/100        # How many hundreds left?
  left  = left - write*100  # Subtract off those hundreds.

  if write > 0
    return 'one hundred'
  end

  write = left/10         # How many tens left?
  left  = left - write*10  # Subtract off those tens.

  if write > 0
    if write == 1  # Uh-oh...
      # Since we can't write "tenty-two"
      # instead of "twelve", we have to
      # make a special exception for these.
      if    left == 0
        num_string = num_string + 'ten'
      elsif left == 1
        num_string = num_string + 'eleven'
```

```
    elsif left == 2
      num_string = num_string + 'twelve'
    elsif left == 3
      num_string = num_string + 'thirteen'
    elsif left == 4
      num_string = num_string + 'fourteen'
    elsif left == 5
      num_string = num_string + 'fifteen'
    elsif left == 6
      num_string = num_string + 'sixteen'
    elsif left == 7
      num_string = num_string + 'seventeen'
    elsif left == 8
      num_string = num_string + 'eighteen'
    elsif left == 9
      num_string = num_string + 'nineteen'
    end

    #  Since we took care of the digit in the
    #  ones place already, we have nothing left to write.

    left = 0
  elsif write == 2
    num_string = num_string + 'twenty'
  elsif write == 3
    num_string = num_string + 'thirty'
  elsif write == 4
    num_string = num_string + 'forty'
  elsif write == 5
    num_string = num_string + 'fifty'
  elsif write == 6
    num_string = num_string + 'sixty'
  elsif write == 7
    num_string = num_string + 'seventy'
  elsif write == 8
    num_string = num_string + 'eighty'
  elsif write == 9
    num_string = num_string + 'ninety'
  end

  if left > 0
    num_string = num_string + '-'
  end
end

write = left  # How many ones left to write out?
left  = 0     # Subtract off those ones.
if write > 0
  if    write == 1
    num_string = num_string + 'one'
  elsif write == 2
    num_string = num_string + 'two'
```

```
    elsif write == 3
      num_string = num_string + 'three'
    elsif write == 4
      num_string = num_string + 'four'
    elsif write == 5
      num_string = num_string + 'five'
    elsif write == 6
      num_string = num_string + 'six'
    elsif write == 7
      num_string = num_string + 'seven'
    elsif write == 8
      num_string = num_string + 'eight'
    elsif write == 9
      num_string = num_string + 'nine'
    end
  end
  if num_string == ''
    #  The only way "num_string" could be empty
    #  is if "number" is 0.
    return 'zero'
  end
  #  If we got this far, then we had a number
  #  somewhere in between 0 and 100, so we need
  #  to return "num_string".
  num_string
end
```

```
puts english_number(  0)
puts english_number(  9)
puts english_number( 10)
puts english_number( 11)
puts english_number( 17)
puts english_number( 32)
puts english_number( 88)
puts english_number( 99)
puts english_number(100)
```

Well, I certainly don't like this program very much. First, it has too much repetition. Second, it doesn't handle numbers greater than 100. Third, it has too many special cases and too many returns. Let's use some arrays and try to clean it up a bit. Plus, we can use recursion for handling large numbers, since when we write out 123,123,123 (giving us "one hundred twenty-three million, one hundred twenty-three thousand, one hundred twenty-three"), we write "one hundred twenty-three" exactly the same three times. So, here we go:

```
def english_number number
  if number < 0  # No negative numbers.
    return 'Please enter a number that isn\'t negative.'
```

```
end
if number == 0
  return 'zero'
end

#  No more special cases!  No more returns!
num_string = ''  #  This is the string we will return.

ones_place = ['one',      'two',      'three',
              'four',     'five',     'six',
              'seven',    'eight',    'nine']
tens_place = ['ten',      'twenty',   'thirty',
              'forty',    'fifty',    'sixty',
              'seventy',  'eighty',   'ninety']
teenagers  = ['eleven',   'twelve',   'thirteen',
              'fourteen', 'fifteen',  'sixteen',
              'seventeen', 'eighteen', 'nineteen']
#  "left" is how much of the number
#          we still have left to write out.
#  "write" is the part we are
#           writing out right now.
#  write and left...get it?  :)
left  = number
write = left/100        #  How many hundreds left?
left  = left - write*100  #  Subtract off those hundreds.

if write > 0
  #  Now here's the recursion:
  hundreds  = english_number write
  num_string = num_string + hundreds + ' hundred'
  if left > 0
    #  So we don't write 'two hundredfifty-one'...
    num_string = num_string + ' '
  end
end

write = left/10         #  How many tens left?
left  = left - write*10  #  Subtract off those tens.

if write > 0
  if ((write == 1) and (left > 0))
    #  Since we can't write "tenty-two" instead of
    #  "twelve", we have to make a special exception
    #  for these.
    num_string = num_string + teenagers[left-1]
    #  The "-1" is because teenagers[3] is
    #  'fourteen', not 'thirteen'.
    #  Since we took care of the digit in the
    #  ones place already, we have nothing left to write.
    left = 0
  else
    num_string = num_string + tens_place[write-1]
    #  The "-1" is because tens_place[3] is
```

```
      #  'forty', not 'thirty'.
    end

    if left > 0
      # So we don't write 'sixtyfour'...
      num_string = num_string + '-'
    end
  end

  write = left  # How many ones left to write out?
  left  = 0     # Subtract off those ones.

  if write > 0
    num_string = num_string + ones_place[write-1]
    # The "-1" is because ones_place[3] is
    # 'four', not 'three'.
  end

  # Now we just return "num_string"...
  num_string
end

puts english_number(  0)
puts english_number(  9)
puts english_number( 10)
puts english_number( 11)
puts english_number( 17)
puts english_number( 32)
puts english_number( 88)
puts english_number( 99)
puts english_number(100)
puts english_number(101)
puts english_number(234)
puts english_number(3211)
puts english_number(999999)
puts english_number(1000000000000)
```

```
zero
nine
ten
eleven
seventeen
thirty-two
eighty-eight
ninety-nine
one hundred
one hundred one
two hundred thirty-four
thirty-two hundred eleven
ninety-nine hundred ninety-nine hundred ninety-nine
one hundred hundred hundred hundred hundred hundred
```

Ahhhh...that's much, much better. The program is fairly dense, which is why I put in so many comments. It even works for large numbers, though not quite as nicely as one would hope. For example, I think 'one trillion' would be a nicer return value for that last number, or even 'one million million' (though all three are correct). In fact, you can do that right now....

10.5 A Few More Things to Try

- *Expanded english_number.* First, put in thousands; it should return 'one thousand' instead of (the sad) 'ten hundred' and 'ten thousand' instead of 'one hundred hundred'.

  Now expand upon english_number some more. For example, put in millions so you get 'one million' instead of 'one thousand thousand'. Then try adding billions, trillions, and so on.

- *Wedding number.* How about wedding_number? It should work almost the same as english_number, except it should insert the word *and* all over the place, returning things like 'nineteen hundred and seventy and two', or however wedding invitations are supposed to look. I'd give you more examples, but I don't fully understand it myself. You might need to contact a wedding coordinator to help you. (I'm really just kidding. You don't have to do this one. I didn't even do this one.)

- *"Ninety-nine Bottles of Beer on the Wall."* Using english_number and your old program on page 49, write out the lyrics to this song the *right* way this time. Punish your computer: have it start at 9999. (Don't pick a number too large, though, because writing all of that to the screen takes your computer quite a while. A hundred thousand bottles of beer takes some time; and if you pick a million, you'll be punishing yourself as well!)

## CHAPTER 11

Reading and Writing, Saving and Loading, Yin and…Something Else

Now if you were sitting here next to me, you'd probably ask why I didn't put on any clothes before you came over. (Well, I didn't know you were coming; you weren't here like ten seconds ago.) But if you had given more warning and I was wearing clothes, you'd be more likely to say something like, "Chris" (and it's a good thing you started with my name, because as anyone near and dear to me will tell you, it's best to make sure you have my attention *before* striking up a conversation, lest I interrupt you 45 seconds later with, "You aren't talking to me, are you? Uh…eel paste in your chair…*what?*"). "Chris," you might say, "I still can't write a program that really *does* anything."

And I'd say, "Yep."

11.1 Doing Something

So far, after your program is done running, there's really no evidence that it ever ran (aside from your memory of it). Nothing on your computer has been changed at all. The least I can do is show how to save the output of your program. For example, let's say you wanted to save the output of your nifty new "99 Bottles of Beer on the Wall" program. All you have to do is add a little bit onto the command line when you run it:

ruby 99bottles.rb > lyrics.txt

That's not even really programming; that's just a command-line trick. And it's not a terribly exciting one, since you can't really use it for a program with any kind of interactivity or to save to more than one file or to save at a time other than the end of the program…. But, hey—it's something. What's happening is that all of the program's output (from all of the putses) is being grabbed and funneled to the named file instead of being printed on your screen.

11.2 The Thing About Computers…

Before we get to real saving and loading, you and I need to talk about something. Something important. It's about computers. The thing about computers—desktops, laptops, cell phones, you name it—is that, well, they suck. This is not by nature, mind you—it isn't intrinsic—and I yearn for the day when they won't suck. But for the moment, by (poor) design, they do. This is most powerfully seen when your computer loses a bunch of your information.

A few years back I was working on a project (thankfully I was the only one on the project at the time). To make a long story short, I dropped the database. All of the information in the database—gone. The very structure of the database (which was itself days and days of work for me)—gone. It was all just gone. It felt like Scotty had beamed up my stomach but forgot the rest of me. I walked around for several hours, just feeling sick, not punching things that would certainly have injured my hand, muttering, "I can't believe I dropped the database…." It was horrible. You know how I did it? It was a mouse-click about 15 pixels too high, followed by a totally reflexive (at that point) hitting of the OK button on the confirmation pop-up. And it was all gone.

User error, you say? Yeah, I suppose it was. I certainly blamed myself. But at some point you have to ask yourself, why is it so fast and so easy to screw things up so catastrophically? At some point you have to start blaming the computer.

Anyway, I'm telling you this because now that your programs can actually do something, it means they can do something *bad*. Now you have to be careful. Make backups. Make them on different computers if you can. Look into source code management systems. (I use Mercurial, and I love it.) I tend to favor things like Gmail, where I can use it from any machine (just in case my main computer melts…it happened once, with actual melting) and where it's someone else's job to make sure I don't lose anything important.

From this point on, just be careful, OK?

11.3 Saving and Loading for Grown-Ups

Now that you're good and afraid, let's get to it. A file is basically just a sequence of bytes. A string is also, ultimately, just a sequence of bytes. This makes saving strings to files pretty easy, at least conceptually. (And Ruby makes it pretty easy in practice.)

Here's a quick example where we save a simple string to a file and then read it back out again. (I'll just show you the program first, and then I'll talk some more about it.)

```
#  The filename doesn't have to end
#  with ".txt", but since it is valid
#  text, why not?
filename    = 'ListerQuote.txt'
test_string = 'I promise that I swear absolutely that ' +
              'I will never mention gazpacho soup again.'

#  The 'w' here is for write-access to the file,
#  since we are trying to write to it.
File.open filename, 'w' do |f|
  f.write test_string
end

read_string = File.read filename

puts(read_string == test_string)
```

```
true
```

File.open is how you open a file, of course. It creates the file object, calls it f (because that's what we said to call it), runs all the code until it gets to the end, and then closes the file. When you open a file, you always have to close it again. In most programming languages you have to remember to do this, but Ruby takes care of it for you at the end. Reading files is even easier than writing them; with File.read Ruby takes care of everything behind the scenes. (I'm not sure why they made writing more complicated, but we'll fix that in just a bit.)

Well, that's all well and good if all you want to save and load are single strings. But what if you wanted to save an array of strings? Or an array of integers and floats? And what about all of the other classes of objects that we don't even cover until the next chapter? *What about the bunnies?*

All right, one thing at a time. Now we can definitely save any kind of object, just as long as we have some well-defined way of converting from a general object to a string and back again. So, maybe an array would be represented as text separated by commas. But what if you wanted to save a string with commas? Well, maybe you could escape the commas somehow….

Figuring this all out would take us a ridiculous amount of time. I mean, it's pretty cool that you can do it at all, but you didn't pay good money for "pretty cool." No sir, this is a De-Luxe-Supremium book you have here. And for that, my friend, we need some serious saving. We need some full-frontal loading. Yes, when you're looking for De-Luxe-Supremium, you want YAML.

11.4 YAML

What is YAML? To know what YAML is, you have to see it for yourself. Or you could see a movie about it. Or I could just tell you.

The thing with geeky acronyms is that they are often recursive (which, hey, that's pretty cute, you've got to admit) and rarely informative (as likely to tell you what they *aren't* as what they are). Take LINUX, for example: Linux Is Not Uncle Xenophobe. There you go. Anyway, I think YAML stands for Yaml Ate My Landlord.

YAML is a format for representing objects as strings. You can use other formats, but YAML is nice because it's human-readable (and human-editable) as well as computer-readable. My wife actually writes YAML all the time, right there in her text editor. Then another program reads it in later. Pretty cool.

YAML is not actually part of the Ruby core (it is its own thing, and many other languages can use YAML), but it is part of the standard distribution. What does that mean? Well, when you install Ruby, you install YAML, too. But if you want to actually use YAML, you'll need to import it into your program. This is really easy, though, with the require method.

```
require 'yaml'  #  Told you it was easy.

test_array = ['Give Quiche A Chance',
              'Mutants Out!',
              'Chameleonic Life-Forms, No Thanks']

#  Here's half of the magic:
test_string = test_array.to_yaml
#  You see?  Kind of like "to_s", and it is in fact a string,
#  but it's a YAML description of "test_array".

filename = 'RimmerTShirts.txt'

File.open filename, 'w' do |f|
  f.write test_string
end

read_string = File.read filename

#  And the other half of the magic:
read_array = YAML::load read_string

puts(read_string == test_string)
puts(read_array  == test_array )
```

```
true
true
```

Simple. Just two extra lines of code (well, three if you count the require line at the top). So, I'm sure the question burning in all of our hearts is "What does the YAML string look like?!" Run it yourself, and you'll see this in RimmerTShirts.txt:

```
---
- Give Quiche A Chance
- Mutants Out!
- "Chameleonic Life-Forms, No Thanks"
```

Pretty clear. I'm not sure why that last line is in double quotes—perhaps because of the dash? I wouldn't be surprised if leaving out the quotes worked, too; YAML is very forgiving...I think it added the quotes only for our benefit. (A quick check says yes, indeed, we can leave those quotes out.)

Wait a second...I said we were saving and loading only one string. But that file has four lines in it. What, one may be well-justified in asking, gives?

Well, it is one string. It's a four-line string. How does a string get to have four lines? It has three *newline characters*. You can add newline characters to strings by just hitting Enter in your code and continuing your string on the next line, though that doesn't play well with proper indentation and ends up looking ugly. There are somewhat less ugly ways of dealing with it, but they require a different way of defining strings. When we want to make a string, we enclose some text in single quotes, and *viola!* A string. But there are other ways—like, five other ways—to define strings. I don't even know what they all are. To learn them all, there are great references out there (I'll point them out in Chapter 15, *Beyond This Fine Book*, on page 123), but in the meantime, let's just learn one more that is commonly used....

11.5 Diversion: Double-Quoted Strings

So far, we've used only single-quoted strings. They are the easiest to use, in the same sense that a shovel is easier to use than a backhoe: when the job gets big enough, it stops being easier.

Consider multiline strings:

```
buffy_quote_1 = '\'Kiss rocks\'?
                 Why would anyone want to kiss...
                 Oh, wait. I get it.'
buffy_quote_2 = "'Kiss rocks'?\n" +
                "Why would anyone want to kiss...\n" +
                "Oh, wait. I get it."
puts buffy_quote_1
puts
puts(buffy_quote_1 == buffy_quote_2)
```

```
'Kiss rocks'?
              Why would anyone want to kiss...
              Oh, wait. I get it.

false
```

Using double quotes, we can indent the strings so they all line up. You'll notice the "\n", which is the escape sequence for the newline character. With this, you can also put a multiline string on one line of code:

```
puts "3...\n2...\n1...\nHAPPY NEW YEAR!"
```

```
3...
2...
1...
HAPPY NEW YEAR!
```

But it doesn't work with the simpler single-quoted strings:

```
puts '3...\n2...\n1...\nHAPPY NEW YEAR!'
```

```
3...\n2...\n1...\nHAPPY NEW YEAR!
```

And just as you must escape single quotes in single-quoted strings (but not double quotes), you must escape double quotes in double-quoted strings (but not single quotes):

```
puts 'single (\') and double (") quotes'
puts "single (') and double (\") quotes"
```

```
single (') and double (") quotes
single (') and double (") quotes
```

So, that's double-quoted strings. In most cases, I prefer the simplicity of single-quoted strings, honestly. But there's one thing that double-quoted strings do very nicely: interpolation. It's sort of a cross between string addition, to_s conversion, and salsa. (The food or the dance—pick whichever metaphor works best for you.)

```
name = 'Luke'
zip  = 90210

puts "Name = #{name}, Zipcode = #{zip}"
```

```
Name = Luke, Zipcode = 90210
```

Snazzy, no? We got to use the variable names right in the string, just by putting it inside "#{...}". And you'll notice that we didn't have to say zip.to_s to convert the ZIP code to a string; Ruby knows that you want it to be a string in this case, so it does the conversion for you.

But it gets even better! You're not limited to variables when using string inter-polation—you can use any expression you want! Ruby evaluates the expression for you, converts to string, and injects the result into the surrounding string:

```
puts "#{2 * 10**4 + 1} Leagues Under the Sea, THE REVENGE!"
```

```
20001 Leagues Under the Sea, THE REVENGE!
```

Good stuff. (Don't say I never gave you nothing.)

11.6 Back to Our Regularly Scheduled Programming

Now where were we? Ah, yes, YAML. As I was saying, YAML takes (or returns) a multiline string. Go ahead and play around with your YAML code. Get familiar with it. Toss in some arrays within arrays; try to fool it with the integer 42 as opposed to the string '42' or with the true object as opposed to the string 'true'. YAML is pretty smart and, if I may be so bold, darned convenient.

You know what would be even better, though? It would be cool if I could just save an object with one method call, just one line of code. And it'd be cool if I could load with just one method call, too. Check it, yo!

```
require 'yaml'
#  First we define these fancy methods...
def yaml_save object, filename
  File.open filename, 'w' do |f|
    f.write(object.to_yaml)
  end
end
def yaml_load filename
  yaml_string = File.read filename

  YAML::load yaml_string
end
#  ...and now we use these fancy methods.
test_array = ['Slick Shoes',
              'Bully Blinders',
              'Pinchers of Peril']

#  Hey, time for some "me" trivia:
#  In Portland once, I met the guy who
#  played Troy's dad.  True story.
filename = 'DatasGadgets.txt'

#  We save it...
yaml_save test_array, filename

#  We load it...
read_array = yaml_load filename

#  We weep for the po' fools that ain't got it...
puts(read_array == test_array)
```

```
true
```

Who's your daddy? Or at the very least an acquaintance of his? Or maybe just knows that you have a daddy? That's right, baby, it's me.

11.7 Renaming Your Photos

Let's do something really useful now. A day ago I got an email from someone wanting to know how to rename a bunch of files. A year ago my wife wanted a program to download the pictures from her camera's memory card and rename them. I'll show you a modified version of her program.

But first, we ought to talk about a few new methods we'll be using in this program. The first is the Dir[] method. We've seen [] used with arrays before...you did know that was a method, didn't you? Oh, yeah, it sure is. You say "arr[2]" and I say "arr.[] 2"—it's all the same.

Anyway, rather than using an array's [] method, we're using the object Dir's [] method. (The Dir is for *directory*.) And instead of passing in a number, like with arrays, this time you pass in a string. This is not just any string; it's a string describing which filenames you are looking for. It then searches for those files and returns an array of the filenames (strings) it found.

For simplicity, I'm just going to say "filename" when I really mean "absolute or relative path and filename."

The format of the input string is pretty easy. It's basically just a filename with a few extra goodies. In fact, if you just pass in a filename, you'll get either an array containing the filename (if the file exists) or an empty array (if it doesn't).

```
puts Dir['ParisHilton.jpg']
```

Naturally, it didn't find anything...what kind of programmer do you think I am?

There are more things you can do with Dir[]; I don't even know what they all are. This will be enough for us, though.

Anyway, I could search for all JPEGs with Dir['*.jpg']. Actually, since these are case-sensitive searches, I should probably include the all-caps version as well, Dir['*.{JPG,jpg}'], which roughly means "Find me all files starting with whatever and ending with a dot and either JPG or jpg." Of course, that searches for JPEGs only in the *current working directory*, which (unless you change it) is the directory you ran the program from. To search in the parent directory, you'd want something like Dir['../*.{JPG,jpg}']. If you wanted to search in the current directory and all subdirectories (a recursive search), you'd want something like Dir['**/*.{JPG,jpg}'].

And remember I said you could change your current working directory? You do that with Dir.chdir; just pass in the path to your new working directory.

We'll also be using File.rename. It should be fairly obvious how it works. I have one thing to say about renaming, though. According to your computer, moving a file and renaming a file are really the same task. Often, only one of these is presented as an option. And, if you think about, this kind of makes sense. If you rename a file from ThingsToWrite/book.txt to ThingsToRead/book.txt, you just moved that file. And if you move a file to the same location, but with a different name, you have renamed it.

The last new method we'll be using is print, which is almost exactly like puts, except it doesn't advance to the next line. I don't use it that often, but it's nice for making little progress bars and things.

Finally, let me tell you a bit about my wife's computer. It's a Windows machine, so the absolute paths are going to be C:/is/for/cook.ie and such. Also, her F:/ drive is really her card reader for her camera's memory card. We're going to move the files to a folder on her hard disk and rename them as we do so. (And since, as we all know, move and rename are the same thing, we'll do this in one fell swoop. Fell stroke? How does that go?)

Yes, I'm using forward slashes. Yes, Windows uses backslashes. Yes, it's perfectly OK to use forward slashes in Ruby. This helps make Ruby programs more cross-platform (though obviously not this one—it runs only on Katy's machine).

```ruby
#  For Katy, with love.

#  (I always write little notes in the programs
#  I write for her.  I deleted all of the dirty
#  ones, though, so that one is all that's left.)

#  This is where she stores her pictures before
#  she gets her YAML on and moves them to the server.
#  Just for my own convenience, I'll go there now.
Dir.chdir 'C:/Documents and Settings/Katy/PictureInbox'

#  First we find all of the pictures to be moved.
pic_names = Dir['F:/**/*.{JPG,jpg}']

puts 'What would you like to call this batch?'
batch_name = gets.chomp

puts
print "Downloading #{pic_names.length} files:  "

#  This will be our counter.  We'll start at 1 today,
#  though normally I like to count from 0.
pic_number = 1

pic_names.each do |name|
  print '.'  #  This is our "progress bar".

  new_name = if pic_number < 10
    "#{batch_name}0#{pic_number}.jpg"
  else
    "#{batch_name}#{pic_number}.jpg"
  end
```

```
# This renames the picture, but since "name"
# has a big long path on it, and "new_name"
# doesn't, it also moves the file to the
# current working directory, which is now
# Katy's PictureInbox folder.
# Since it's a *move*, this effectively
# downloads and deletes the originals.
# And since this is a memory card, not a
# hard drive, each of these takes a second
# or so; hence, the little dots let her
# know that my program didn't hose her machine.
# (Some marriage advice from your favorite
# author/programmer:  it's all about the
# little things.)
```

The first time I wrote this program, I forgot that little line that increments the counter. What happened? It copied every picture to the same new filename… *over* the previous picture! This effectively deleted every picture except for the last one to be copied. Good thing I always, always, always make backups. Because, you know, the thing about computers….

```
# Now where were we?  Oh, yeah...
  File.rename name, new_name
    # Finally, we increment the counter.
  pic_number = pic_number + 1
end

puts  # This is so we aren't on progress bar line.
puts 'Done, cutie!'
```

Nice! Of course, the full program I wrote for her also downloads the movies, deletes the thumbnails from the camera (since only the camera can use them), extracts the time and date from the actual .jpg or .avi file, and renames the file using that. It also makes sure *never* to copy over an existing file. Yep, it's a pretty fancy program, but that's for another day.

11.8 A Few Things to Try

- *Safer picture downloading.* Adapt the picture-downloading/file-renaming program to your computer by adding some safety features to make sure you never overwrite a file. A few methods you might find useful are File.exist? (pass it a filename, and it will return true or false) and exit (like if return and Napoleon had a baby—it kills your program right where it stands; this is good for spitting out an error message and then quitting).

- *Build your own playlist.* For this to work, you need to have some music ripped to your computer in some format. We've ripped a 100 or so CDs, and we keep them in directories something like music/genre/artist_and_cd_name/track_number.ogg. (I'm partial to the .ogg format, though this would work just as well with .mp3s or whatever you use.)

  Building a playlist is easy. It's just a regular text file (no YAML required, even). Each line is a filename, like this:

```
music/world/Stereolab--Margarine_Eclipse/track05.ogg
```

What makes it a playlist? Well, you have to give the file the .m3u extension, like playlist.m3u or something. And that's all a playlist is: a text file with an .m3u extension.

So, have your program search for various music files and build you a playlist. Use your shuffle method on page 75 to mix up your playlist. Then check it out in your favorite music player (Winamp, MPlayer, and so on)!

- *Build a better playlist.* After listening to playlists for a while, you might start to find that a purely random shuffle just doesn't quite seem...mixed up enough. (*Random* and *mixed up* are not at all the same thing. Random is totally clumpy.) For example, here's an excerpt from a playlist I made a while back of Thelonius Monk and Faith No More:

```
music/Jazz/Monk--Nutty/track08.ogg
music/Jazz/Monk--London_Collection_1/track05.ogg
music/Jazz/Monk--Nutty/track13.ogg
music/Jazz/Monk--Round_Midnight/track02.ogg
music/Jazz/Monk--Round_Midnight/track14.ogg
music/Jazz/Monk--Round_Midnight/track15.ogg
music/Jazz/Monk--Round_Midnight/track08.ogg
music/Rock/FNM--Who_Cares_A_Lot_2/track02.ogg
music/Rock/FNM--Who_Cares_A_Lot_2/track08.ogg
music/Rock/FNM--Who_Cares_A_Lot_1/track02.ogg
music/Rock/FNM--Who_Cares_A_Lot_2/track01.ogg
```

Hey! I asked for random! Well, that's exactly what I got...but I wanted mixed up. So, here's the grand challenge: instead of using your old shuffle, write a new music_shuffle method. It should take an array of filenames (like those listed previously) and mix them up good and proper.

You'll probably need to use the split method for strings. It returns an array of chopped-up pieces of the original string, split where you specify, like this:

```
awooga = 'this/is/not/a/daffodil'.split '/'
puts awooga
```

```
this
is
not
a
daffodil
```

Mix it up as best you can!

## CHAPTER 12

New Classes of Objects

So far we've seen several kinds, or *classes*, of objects: strings, integers, floats, arrays, a few special objects (true, false, and nil), and so on. In Ruby, these class names are always capitalized: String, Integer, Float, Array, File, and Dir. (You remember back on page 85 when we asked the File class to open a file for us, and it handed us back an actual file, which we called, in a fit of rabid creativity, f? Those were the days.... Anyway, we never ended up needing an actual directory object from Dir, but we could have gotten one if we had asked nicely.)

File.open was a mildly unusual way to get an object from a class. In general, you'll use the new method:

```
alpha = Array.new  + [12345]  #  Array addition.
beta  = String.new + 'hello'  #  String addition.
karma = Time.new              #  Current date and time.

puts "alpha = #{alpha}"
puts "beta  = #{beta}"
puts "karma = #{karma}"
```

```
alpha = 12345
beta  = hello
karma = Tue Sep 27 14:57:58 -0400 2011
```

Because we can create array and string *literals* using [...] and '...', we rarely create them using new. (Though it might not be clear from the example there, String.new creates an empty string, and Array.new creates an empty array.) Also, numbers are special exceptions: you can't create an integer with Integer.new. (Which one would it create, you know?) You can make one only using an integer literal (just writing it out as you've been doing).

12.1 The Time Class

What's the story with this Time class? Time objects represent (you guessed it) moments in time. You can add (or subtract) numbers to (or from) times to get new times; adding 1.5 to a time makes a new time one-and-a-half seconds later:

```ruby
time  = Time.new  #  The moment we ran this code.
time2 = time + 60  #  One minute later.

puts time
puts time2
```

```
Tue Sep 27 14:57:58 -0400 2011
Tue Sep 27 14:58:58 -0400 2011
```

You can also make a time for a specific moment using Time.local:

```ruby
puts Time.local(2000, 1, 1)          #  Y2K.
puts Time.local(1976, 8, 3, 13, 31)  #  When I was born.
```

```
Sat Jan 01 00:00:00 -0500 2000
Tue Aug 03 13:31:00 -0400 1976
```

You'll notice the -0400 and -0500 in these times. That's to account for the difference between the local time and Greenwich mean time (GMT, the One True Time Zone, dontcha know). This can be because of being in a different time zone or daylight saving time or who knows what else. So, you can see that I was born in daylight saving time, while it was *not* daylight saving time when Y2K struck. (By the way, the parentheses are to group the parameters to local together; otherwise, puts might start thinking those are its parameters.) The more parameters you add to local, the more accurate your time becomes.

On the other hand, if you want to avoid time zones and daylight saving time altogether and just use GMT, there's always Time.gm.

```ruby
puts Time.gm(1955, 11, 5) #  A red-letter day.
```

```
Sat Nov 05 00:00:00 UTC 1955
```

You can compare times using the comparison methods (an earlier time is *less than* a later time), and if you subtract one time from another, you'll get the number of seconds between them. Play around with it!

If you happen to be using an older version of Ruby, there's this problem with the Time class. It thinks the world began at *epoch*: the stroke of midnight, January 1, 1970, GMT. I don't really know of any satisfying way of explaining this, but here goes: at some point, probably before I was even born, some people (Unix folks, I believe) decided that a good way to represent time on computers was to count the number of seconds since the very beginning of the 70s. So, time "zero" stood for the birth of that great decade, and they called it *epoch*.

Now this was all long before Ruby. In those ancient days (and programming in those ancient languages), you often had to worry about your numbers getting too large. In general, a number would either be from 0 to around 4 billion or be from -2 billion to +2 billion, depending on how they chose to store it.

For whatever reasons (compatibility, tradition, cruelty…whatever), older versions of Ruby decided to go with these conventions. So (and this is the important point), you *couldn't have times more than 2 billion seconds away from epoch!* This restriction wasn't too painful, though, because this span is from sometime in December 1901 to sometime in January 2038.

In all fairness, Ruby did (and still does) provide other classes, such as Date and DateTime, for handling just about any point in history. But these are such a pain to use compared to Time that I don't feel like figuring them out myself, much less teaching them to you. What's the difference between civil time and commercial time? I have no idea. Julian calendar vs. Gregorian calendar? Italian vs. English reform dates? I'm sure there's a Perfectly Good Reason for all that complexity. (In case you weren't sitting across from me as I typed that, I was rolling my eyes.) But anyway, that's fixed in newer versions of Ruby (1.9 and up).

> Presumably this was done because the momentous fashion advances of the time rivaled the birth of Jesus in terms of cultural and spiritual significance…it's Jesus Christ vs. *Jesus Christ Superstar*, and that, my friends, is a tough call.

12.2 A Few Things to Try

- *One billion seconds!* Find out the exact second you were born (if you can). Figure out when you will turn (or perhaps when you did turn) one billion seconds old. Then go mark your calendar.

- *Happy birthday!* Ask what year a person was born in, then the month, and then the day. Figure out how old they are, and give them a big SPANK! for each birthday they have had.

12.3 The Hash Class

Another useful class is the Hash class. Hashes are a lot like arrays: they have a bunch of slots that can point to various objects. However, in an array, the slots are lined up in a row, and each one is numbered (starting from zero). In a hash, the slots aren't in a row (they are just sort of jumbled together), and you can use *any* object to refer to a slot, not just a number. It's good to use hashes when you have a bunch of things you want to keep track of but they don't really fit into an ordered list. For example, we can make a dictionary for little C's vocabulary:

```ruby
dict_array = []  # array literal; same as Array.new
dict_hash  = {}  # hash literal;  same as Hash.new

dict_array[0]       = 'candle'
dict_array[1]       = 'glasses'
dict_array[2]       = 'truck'
dict_array[3]       = 'Alicia'
dict_hash['shia-a'] = 'candle'
dict_hash['shaya' ] = 'glasses'
dict_hash['shasha'] = 'truck'
dict_hash['sh-sha'] = 'Alicia'

dict_array.each do |word|
  puts word
end

dict_hash.each do |c_word, word|
  puts "#{c_word}:  #{word}"
end
```

```
candle
glasses
truck
Alicia
shia-a:  candle
shaya:   glasses
shasha:  truck
sh-sha:  Alicia
```

If I use an array, I have to remember that slot 0 is for "shia-a," slot 1 is for "shaya," and so on. But if I use a hash, it's easy! Slot 'shia-a' holds the word for "shia-a," of course. There's nothing to remember. You might have noticed that when we used each, the objects in the hash didn't come out in the same order we put them in. (I mean, they could, I suppose…it's technically possible. They just don't usually.) Arrays are for keeping things in order; hashes are for keeping things referenced by other things.

Though people usually use strings to name the slots in a hash, you could use any kind of object, even arrays and other hashes. (I have no idea why you'd want to do this, though.)

```ruby
weird_hash = Hash.new

weird_hash[12] = 'monkeys'
weird_hash[[]] = 'emptiness'
weird_hash[Time.new] = 'no time like the present'
```

Hashes and arrays are good for different things; it's up to you to decide which one is best for a particular problem. I probably use hashes at least as often as arrays; they're wonderful.

12.4 Ranges

Range is another great class. Ranges represent intervals of numbers. On the next page is just a quick glance at some of the methods ranges have.

```
# This is your range literal.
letters = 'a'..'c'

# Convert range to array.
puts(['a','b','c'] == letters.to_a)

# Iterate over a range:
('A'..'Z').each do |letter|
  print letter
end
puts

god_bless_the_70s = 1970..1979
puts god_bless_the_70s.min
puts god_bless_the_70s.max
puts(god_bless_the_70s.include?(1979  ))
puts(god_bless_the_70s.include?(1980  ))
puts(god_bless_the_70s.include?(1974.5))
```

```
true
ABCDEFGHIJKLMNOPQRSTUVWXYZ
1970
1979
true
false
true
```

Actually, you can have intervals of letters, strings, times…pretty much anything you can place in order—where you can say things like this < that and such. It's not always clear, though, just what a range of strings is. In practice, I never use ranges over anything but integers.

Do you really need ranges? No, not really. It's the same with hashes and times, I suppose. You can program fairly well without them (and most languages don't have anything like them, anyway). But it's all about style, about intention, and about capturing snapshots of your brain right there in your code.

And this is all just the tip of the iceberg. Each of these classes has way more methods than I have shown you, and this isn't even a tenth of the classes that come with Ruby. But you don't really *need* most of them…they are just time-savers. You can pick them up gradually as you go. That's how most of us do it.

12.5 Stringy Superpowers

I'd really feel like I was doing you a disservice if I didn't show you at least a little more of what strings can do (in Ruby, at least). Plus, if I do, I can give you more interesting exercises. Mind you, I'm still not going to show you even half, but I've just *got* to show you a little more.

Remember back on page 55 when I said a lot of the string methods also work on arrays? Well, it goes both ways: some of the array methods you've learned also work on strings.

Perhaps the most important and versatile is the [...] method. The first thing you can do with it is pass in a number and get the character at that position in the string:

```
da_man = 'Mr. T'
big_T  = da_man[4]
puts big_T
```

```
T
```

And then you can do fun stuff like this:

```
puts "Hello.  My name is Julian."
puts "I'm extremely perceptive."
puts "What's your name?"

name = gets.chomp
puts "Hi, #{name}."

if name[0] == 'C'
  puts 'You have excellent taste in footwear.'
  puts 'I can just tell.'
end
```

```
‹ Hello. My name is Julian.
  I'm extremely perceptive.
  What's your name?
⇒ Chris
‹ Hi, Chris.
  You have excellent taste in footwear.
  I can just tell.
```

This is just the beginning of our friend, the [...] method. Instead of picking out only one character, we can pick out substrings in two ways. One way is to pass in two numbers: the first tells us where to start the substring, and the second tells us how long of a substring we are looking for.

The second way, though, is quite possibly too sexy for your car: just pass in a range.

And both of these ways have a little twist. If you pass in a negative index, it counts from the *end* of the string. Dude!

```
prof = 'We tore the universe a new space-hole, alright!'
puts prof[12,  8]
puts prof[12..19] # 8 characters total
puts
def is_avi? filename
  filename.downcase[-4..-1] == '.avi'
end
#  Vicarious embarrassment.
puts is_avi?('DANCEMONKEYBOY.AVI')
#  Hey, I wasn't even 2 at the time...
puts is_avi?('toilet_paper_fiasco.jpg')
```

```
universe
universe

true
false
```

12.6 A Few More Things to Try

- *Party like it's roman_to_integer 'mcmxcix'!* Come on, you knew it was coming, didn't you? It's the other half of your roman_numeral 1999 method. Make sure to reject strings that aren't valid Roman numerals.

- *Birthday helper!* Write a program to read in names and birth dates from a text file. It should then ask you for a name. You type one in, and it tells you when that person's next birthday will be (and, for the truly adventurous, how old they will be). The input file should look something like this:

```
Christopher Alexander,  Oct  4, 1936
Christopher Lambert,    Mar 29, 1957
Christopher Lee,        May 27, 1922
Christopher Lloyd,      Oct 22, 1938
Christopher Pine,       Aug  3, 1976
Christopher Plummer,    Dec 13, 1927
Christopher Walken,     Mar 31, 1943
The King of Spain,      Jan  5, 1938
```

(That would be *me* Christopher Pine, not the young James T. Kirk; I don't care when he was born.) You'll probably want to break each line up and put it in a hash, using the name as your key and the date as your value. In other words: words:

```
birth_dates['The King of Spain'] = 'Jan 5, 1938'
```

(You can store the date in some other format if you prefer.)

Though you can do it without this tip, your program might look prettier if you use the each_line method for strings. It works pretty much like each does for arrays, but it returns each line of the multiline string one at a time (but with the line endings, so you might need to chomp them). Just thought I'd mention it....

12.7 Classes and the Class Class

I'll warn you right now: this section is a bit of a brain bender, so if you're not feeling particularly strong of stomach, you can skip to the next chapter. At least for now, it's mainly of academic interest. But just in case you were wondering...

As you may have noticed, we can call methods on strings (things such as length and chomp), but we can also call methods on the actual String class, methods such as new. This is because, in Ruby, classes are real objects. (This isn't the case in most languages.) And since every object is in some class, classes must be, too. We can find the class of an object using the class method:

```
puts(42.class)
puts("I'll have mayonnaise on mine!".class)
puts(Time.new.class)  # No shocker here.
puts(Time.class)      # A little more interesting...
puts(String.class)    # Yeah, UK...

# Hold your breath through the tunnel, boys and girls!
puts(Class.class)
# <gasp!>
```

```
Fixnum
String
Time
Class
Class
Class
```

If this makes sense to you right now, then *stop thinking about it!* You might screw it up! Otherwise...don't sweat it too much. Move on; let your subconscious do the work later.

## CHAPTER 13

Creating New Classes, Changing Existing Ones

Back on page 78, we wrote a method to give the English phrase for a given integer. It wasn't an integer method, though; it was just a generic "program" method. Wouldn't it be nice if you could write something like 22.to_eng instead of english_number 22? Here's how:

```
class Integer
  def to_eng
    if self == 5
      english = 'five'
    else
      english = 'forty-two'
    end

    english
  end
end

#  I'd better test on a couple of numbers...
puts 5.to_eng
puts 42.to_eng
```

```
five
forty-two
```

Well, I tested it; it seems to work.

We defined an integer method by jumping into the Integer class, defining the method there, and jumping back out. Now all integers have this (somewhat incomplete) method. In fact, you can do this with any method in any class, even the built-in methods. If you don't like the reverse method for strings, you can just redefine it in much the same way, but I don't recommend it! It's best to leave the old methods alone and to make new ones when you want to do something new.

Confused yet? Let me go over that last program some more. So far, whenever we executed any code or defined any methods, we did it in the default "program" object. In our last program, we left that object for the first time and hopped into the Integer class. We defined a method there (which makes it an integer method), and now all integers can use it. Inside that method we use self to refer to the object (the integer) using the method.

13.1 A Few Things to Try

- *Extend the built-in classes.* How about making your shuffle method on page 75 an array method? Or how about making factorial an integer method? 4.to_roman, anyone? In each case, remember to use self to access the object the method is being called on (the 4 in 4.to_roman).

13.2 Creating Classes

We've now seen a smattering of different classes. However, it's easy to come up with kinds of objects that Ruby doesn't have—objects you'd like it to have. Fear not; creating a new class is as easy as extending an old one. Let's say we wanted to make some dice in Ruby, for example. Here's how we could make the Die class:

```ruby
class Die

  def roll
    1 + rand(6)
  end

end

#  Let's make a couple of dice...
dice = [Die.new, Die.new]

#  ...and roll them.
dice.each do |die|
  puts die.roll
end
```

```
4
2
```

(If you skipped the section on random numbers, rand(6) just gives a random number between 0 and 5.) And that's it! These are objects of our very own. Roll the dice a few times (run the program again), and watch what turns up.

We can define all sorts of methods for our objects...but there's something missing. Working with these objects feels a lot like programming before we learned about variables. Look at our dice, for example. We can roll them, and each time we do they give us a different number. But if we wanted to hang onto that number, we would have to create a variable to point to the number. It seems like any decent die should be able to *have* a number and that rolling the die should change that number. If we keep track of the die, we shouldn't also have to keep track of the number it is showing.

However, if we try to store the number we rolled in a (local) variable in roll, it will be gone as soon as roll is finished. We need to store the number in a different kind of variable, an *instance variable*.

13.3 Instance Variables

Normally when we want to talk about a string, we will just call it a *string*. However, we could also call it a *string object*. Sometimes programmers might call it an *instance* of the class String, but it's just another way of saying *string*. An *instance* of a class is just an object of that class.

So, instance variables are just an object's variables. A method's local variables last until the method is finished. An object's instance variables, on the other hand, will last as long as the object does. To tell instance variables from local variables, they have @ in front of their names:

```ruby
class Die

  def roll
    @number_showing = 1 + rand(6)
  end

  def showing
    @number_showing
  end

end

die = Die.new
die.roll
puts die.showing
puts die.showing
die.roll
puts die.showing
puts die.showing
```

```
1
1
2
2
```

Very nice! roll rolls the die, and showing tells us which number is showing. However, what if we try to look at what's showing before we've rolled the die (before we've set @number_showing)?

```ruby
class Die

  def roll
    @number_showing = 1 + rand(6)
  end

  def showing
    @number_showing
  end
end
# Since I'm not going to use this die again,
# I don't need to save it in a variable.
puts Die.new.showing
```

```
nil
```

Hmmm...well, at least it didn't give us an error. Still, it doesn't really make sense for a die to be "unrolled," or whatever nil is supposed to mean here. It would be nice if we could set up our new Die object right when it's created. That's what initialize is for; as soon as an object is created, initialize is automatically called on it:

```ruby
class Die

  def initialize
    # I'll just roll the die, though we could do something else
    # if we wanted to, such as setting the die to have 6 showing.
    roll
  end

  def roll
    @number_showing = 1 + rand(6)
  end

  def showing
    @number_showing
  end

end

puts Die.new.showing
```

```
6
```

(One thing to note here: in the previous code, we are first just defining what the Die class is by defining the methods initialize, roll, and showing. However, none of these is actually called until the very last line.)

Very nice. Our dice are just about perfect. The only feature that might be missing is a way to set which side of a die is showing...why don't you write a cheat method that does just that? Come back when you're done (and when you tested that it worked, of course). Make sure that someone can't set the die to have a 7 showing; you're cheating, not bending the laws of logic.

13.4 new vs. initialize

That's some pretty cool stuff we just covered. But the relationship between new and initialize is a bit subtle. And "subtle" may as well mean "confusing." Just what is the deal?

The methods new and initialize work hand in hand. You use new to create a new object, and initialize is then called automatically (if you defined it in your class). They pretty much happen at the same time. How do you keep them straight?

First, new is a method of the *class*, while initialize is a method of the *instance*. You use new to create the instance, and then initialize is automatically called on that instance. This means that the call to new must come first! Until you call new, there's no instance to call initialize upon.

Second, you define initialize in your class, but you never define new. (It's already built in to all classes.) Conversely, you call new to create an object, but you never call initialize. The method new takes care of that for you.

(Strictly speaking, it is possible to call initialize, just as it is possible to define new. But doing so is either very advanced or very stupid. Or both. Let's not even go there.)

The reason for having these two methods is that you really need one of them to be a class method and the other to be an instance method. If you think about it, new has to be a class method, because when you want to create an object, the object you want *does not exist yet!* You can't say, for example, the following:

```
die.new
```

because die doesn't exist yet.

And initialize really has to be an instance method, because you are initializing *that object*. This means that you need access to the instance variables and such. You can't do that from a class method, because it wouldn't know which instance to get the instance variables from. (You certainly don't want to initialize every single instance of Die every time you create a new one.)

So just remember, you *define* the *instance* method initialize, and you *call* the *class* method new (and not the other way around).

13.5 Baby Dragon

Great! You know how to create your own classes, even some of the subtle bits, but so far you've really only seen a small, fluffy, toy example. Let me give you something a bit more chewy. Let's say we want to make a simple virtual pet, a baby dragon. Like most babies, it should be able to eat, sleep, and poop, which means we will need to be able to feed it, put it to bed, and take it on walks. Internally, our dragon will need to keep track of whether it is hungry, tired, or needs to go, but we won't be able to see that when we interact with our dragon, just like you can't ask a human baby, "Are you hungry?" We'll also add a few other fun ways we can interact with our baby dragon, and when he is born, we'll give him a name. (Whatever you pass into the new method is then passed onto the initialize method for you.) OK, let's give it a shot:

```ruby
class Dragon

  def initialize name
    @name = name
    @asleep = false
    @stuff_in_belly    - 10  # He's full.
    @stuff_in_intestine =  0  # He doesn't need to go.

    puts "#{@name} is born."
  end

  def feed
    puts "You feed #{@name}."
    @stuff_in_belly = 10
    passage_of_time
  end

  def walk
    puts "You walk #{@name}."
    @stuff_in_intestine = 0
    passage_of_time
  end

  def put_to_bed
    puts "You put #{@name} to bed."
    @asleep = true
    3.times do
      if @asleep
        passage_of_time
      end
      if @asleep
        puts "#{@name} snores, filling the room with smoke."
```

```ruby
      end
    end
    if @asleep
      @asleep = false
      puts "#{@name} wakes up slowly."
    end
  end

  def toss
    puts "You toss #{@name} up into the air."
    puts 'He giggles, which singes your eyebrows.'
    passage_of_time
  end
  def rock
    puts "You rock #{@name} gently."
    @asleep = true
    puts 'He briefly dozes off...'
    passage_of_time
    if @asleep
      @asleep = false
      puts '...but wakes when you stop.'
    end
  end

  private
  #  "private" means that the methods defined here are
  #  methods internal to the object.  (You can feed your
  #  dragon, but you can't ask him whether he's hungry.)
  def hungry?
    #  Method names can end with "?".
    #  Usually, we do this only if the method
    #  returns true or false, like this:
    @stuff_in_belly <= 2
  end

  def poopy?
    @stuff_in_intestine >= 8
  end

  def passage_of_time
    if @stuff_in_belly > 0
      #  Move food from belly to intestine.
      @stuff_in_belly    = @stuff_in_belly    - 1
      @stuff_in_intestine = @stuff_in_intestine + 1
    else  #  Our dragon is starving!
      if @asleep
        @asleep = false
        puts 'He wakes up suddenly!'
      end
      puts "#{@name} is starving!  In desperation, he ate YOU!"
      exit  #  This quits the program.
    end
```

```
      if @stuff_in_intestine >= 10
        @stuff_in_intestine = 0
        puts "Whoops!  #{@name} had an accident..."
      end

      if hungry?
        if @asleep
          @asleep = false
          puts 'He wakes up suddenly!'
        end
        puts "#{@name}'s stomach grumbles..."
      end

      if poopy?
        if @asleep
          @asleep = false
          puts 'He wakes up suddenly!'
        end
        puts "#{@name} does the potty dance..."
      end
    end

end

pet = Dragon.new 'Norbert'
pet.feed
pet.toss
pct.walk
pet.put_to_bed
pet.rock
pet.put_to_bed
pet.put_to_bed
pet.put_to_bed
pet.put_to_bed
```

```
Norbert is born.
You feed Norbert.
You toss Norbert up into the air.
He giggles, which singes your eyebrows.
You walk Norbert.
You put Norbert to bed.
Norbert snores, filling the room with smoke.
Norbert snores, filling the room with smoke.
Norbert snores, filling the room with smoke.
Norbert wakes up slowly.
You rock Norbert gently.
He briefly dozes off...
...but wakes when you stop.
You put Norbert to bed.
He wakes up suddenly!
Norbert's stomach grumbles...
You put Norbert to bed.
He wakes up suddenly!
```

```
Norbert's stomach grumbles...
You put Norbert to bed.
He wakes up suddenly!
```

```
Norbert's stomach grumbles...
Norbert does the potty dance...
You put Norbert to bed.
He wakes up suddenly!
Norbert is starving! In desperation, he ate YOU!
```

Whew! Of course, it would be nicer if this were an interactive program...oh, I think I smell an exercise coming on.

We saw a few new things in that example. The first is the word private that we stuck right in the middle of our class definition. I could have left it out, but I wanted to enforce the idea that certain methods are things you can do to a dragon and other methods are used only within the dragon. You can think of these as being "under the hood": unless you are an automobile mechanic, all you really need to know is the gas pedal, the brake pedal, and the steering wheel. A programmer might call those the *public interface* of your car. How your airbag knows when to deploy, however, is internal to the car; the typical user (driver) doesn't need to know how that works.

Actually, for a bit more concrete example along those lines, let's talk about how you might represent a car in a video game. First, you would want to decide what you want your public interface to look like; in other words, which methods should people be able to call on one of your car objects? Well, they need to be able to push the gas pedal and the brake pedal, but they would also need to be able to specify how hard they are pushing the pedal. (There's a big difference between flooring it and tapping it.) They would also need to be able to steer, and again, they would need to be able to say how hard they are turning the wheel. I suppose you could go further and add a clutch, turn signals, rocket launcher, afterburner, flux capacitor, and so on.... It depends on what type of game you are making.

Internal to a car object, though, much more would need to be going on; other things a car would need are a speed, a direction, and a position (at the most basic). These attributes would be modified by pressing on the gas or brake pedals and turning the wheel, of course, but the user would not be able to set the position directly (which would be like warping). You might also want to keep track of skidding or damage, whether you have caught any air, and so on. These would all be internal to your car object (that is, not directly accessible by the player; these would be private).

13.6 A Few More Things to Try

- *Orange tree.* Make an OrangeTree class that has a height method that returns its height and a one_year_passes method that, when called, ages the tree one year. Each year the tree grows taller (however much you think an orange tree should grow in a year), and after some number of years (again, your call) the tree should die. For the first few years, it should not produce fruit, but after a while it should, and I guess that older trees produce more each year than younger trees...whatever you think makes the most sense. And, of course, you should be able to count_the_oranges (which returns the number of oranges on the tree) and pick_an_orange (which reduces the @orange_count by 1 and returns a string telling you how delicious the orange was, or else it just tells you that there are no more oranges to pick this year). Make sure any oranges you don't pick one year fall off before the next year.

- *Interactive baby dragon.* Write a program that lets you enter commands such as *feed* and *walk* and calls those methods on your dragon. Of course, since you are inputting just strings, you will need some sort of *method dispatch*, where your program checks which string was entered and then calls the appropriate method.

## CHAPTER 14

Blocks and Procs

This is definitely one of the coolest features of Ruby. Some other languages have this feature, though they may call it something else (like *closures*), but most of the more popular ones don't, and it's a shame. And, in any case, Ruby makes it so pretty with its cute little syntax!

What is this cool new thing? It's the ability to take a *block* of code (code in between do and end), wrap it up in an object (called a *proc*), store it in a variable or pass it to a method, and run the code in the block whenever you feel like it (more than once, if you want). So, it's kind of like a method itself, except it isn't bound to an object (it *is* an object), and you can store it or pass it around like you can with any object. I think it's example time:

```
toast = Proc.new do
  puts 'Cheers!'
end

toast.call
toast.call
toast.call
```

```
Cheers!
Cheers!
Cheers!
```

I created a proc (which I think is supposed to be short for *procedure*, but far more important, it rhymes with *block*) that held the block of code, and then I called the proc three times. As you can see, it's a lot like a method.

Actually, it's even more like a method than I have shown you, because blocks can take parameters:

```
do_you_like = Proc.new do |good_stuff|
  puts "I *really* like #{good_stuff}!"
end
```

```
do_you_like.call 'chocolate'
do_you_like.call 'Ruby'
```

```
I *really* like chocolate!
I *really* like Ruby!
```

OK, so we see what blocks and procs are, and how to use them, but what's the point? Why not just use methods? Well, it's because there are some things you just can't do with methods. In particular, you can't pass methods into other methods (but you can pass procs into methods), and methods can't return other methods (but they can return procs). This is simply because procs are objects; methods aren't.

(By the way, is any of this looking familiar? Yep, you've seen blocks before...when you learned about iterators. But let's talk more about that in a bit.)

14.1 Methods That Take Procs

When we pass a proc into a method, we can control how, if, or how many times we call the proc. For example, let's say we want to do something before and after some code is run:

```
def do_self_importantly some_proc
  puts "Everybody just HOLD ON!  I'm doing something..."
  some_proc.call
  puts "OK everyone, I'm done.  As you were."
end

say_hello = Proc.new do
  puts 'hello'
end

say_goodbye = Proc.new do
  puts 'goodbye'
end

do_self_importantly say_hello
do_self_importantly say_goodbye
```

```
Everybody just HOLD ON!  I'm doing something...
hello
OK everyone, I'm done.  As you were.
Everybody just HOLD ON!  I'm doing something...
goodbye
OK everyone, I'm done.  As you were.
```

Maybe that doesn't appear particularly fabulous...but it is. It's all too common in programming to have strict requirements about what must be done when. Remember opening and closing a file? If you want to save or load a file, you have to open the file, write or read the relevant data, and then close the file. If you forget to close the file, Bad Things can happen. But each time you want to save or load a file, you have to do the same thing: open the file, do what you *really* want to do, and then close the file. It's tedious and easy to forget. But with this trick, it's not even an issue.

You can also write methods that will determine how many times (or even *whether*) to call a proc. Here's a method that will call the proc passed in about half of the time and another that will call it twice:

```ruby
def maybe_do some_proc
  if rand(2) == 0
    some_proc.call
  end
end

def twice_do some_proc
  some_proc.call
  some_proc.call
end

wink = Proc.new do
  puts '<wink>'
end

glance = Proc.new do
  puts '<glance>'
end

maybe_do wink
maybe_do wink
maybe_do glance
maybe_do glance
twice_do wink
twice_do glance
```

```
<wink>
<wink>
<glance>
<wink>
<wink>
<glance>
<glance>
```

These are some of the more common uses of procs that enable us to do things we simply could not have done using methods alone. Sure, you could write a method to wink twice, and you could do it with your left pinky! But you couldn't write one to just do *something* twice.

Before we move on, let's look at one last example. So far the procs we have passed in have been fairly similar to each other. This time they will be quite different, so you can see how much such a method depends on the procs passed into it. Our method will take some object and a proc and will call the proc on that object. If the proc returns false, we quit; otherwise, we call the proc with the returned object. We keep doing this until the proc returns false (which it had better do eventually, or the program will crash). The method will return the last non-false value returned by the proc.

```ruby
def do_until_false first_input, some_proc
  input  = first_input
  output = first_input

  while output
    input  = output
    output = some_proc.call input
  end

  input
end

build_array_of_squares = Proc.new do |array|
  last_number = array.last
  if last_number <= 0
    false
  else
    #  Take off the last number...
    array.pop
    #  ...and replace it with its square...
    array.push last_number*last_number
    #  ...followed by the next smaller number.
    array.push last_number-1
  end
end

always_false = Proc.new do |just_ignore_me|
  false
end

puts do_until_false([5], build_array_of_squares).inspect

yum = 'lemonade with a hint of orange blossom water'
puts do_until_false(yum, always_false)
```

```
[25, 16, 9, 4, 1, 0]
lemonade with a hint of orange blossom water
```

OK, so that was a pretty weird example, I'll admit. But it shows how differently our method acts when given very different procs. (Do yourself a favor, and try that lemonade. Unbelievable.)

The inspect method is a lot like to_s, except the string it returns tries to show you the Ruby code for building the object you passed it. Here it shows us the whole array returned by our first call to do_until_false. Also, you might notice that we never actually squared that 0 on the end of that array, but since 0 squared is still just 0, we didn't have to do this. And since always_false was, you know, always false, do_until_false didn't do anything at all the second time we called it; it just returned what was passed in.

14.2 Methods That Return Procs

One of the cool things you can do with procs is create them in methods and return them. This allows all sorts of crazy programming power (things with impressive names, such as *lazy evaluation*, *infinite data structures*, and *currying*). I don't actually do these things very often, but they are just about the sexiest programming techniques around.

In this example, compose takes two procs and returns a new proc that, when called, calls the first proc and passes its result into the second:

```
def compose proc1, proc2
  Proc.new do |x|
    proc2.call(proc1.call(x))
  end
end

square_it = Proc.new do |x|
  x * x
end

double_it = Proc.new do |x|
  x + x
end

double_then_square = compose double_it, square_it
square_then_double = compose square_it, double_it

puts double_then_square.call(5)
puts square_then_double.call(5)
```

```
100
50
```

(Notice that the call to proc1 had to be inside the parentheses for proc2 in order for it to run first.)

14.3 Passing Blocks (Not Procs) into Methods

OK, so this has been more theoretically cool than actually cool, partly because this is all a bit of a hassle to use. I'm man enough to admit that. A lot of the problem is that we have to go through three steps (defining the method, making the proc, and calling the method with the proc) when it sort of feels like there should be only two (defining the method and passing the *block* of code right into the method, without using a proc at all), since most of the time you don't want to use the proc/block after you pass it into the method. It should be...more like how iterators work! Sho' nuff, baby:

```ruby
class Array

  def each_even(&was_a_block__now_a_proc)
    # We start with "true" because
    # arrays start with 0, which is even.
    is_even = true

    self.each do |object|
      if is_even
        was_a_block__now_a_proc.call object
      end

      # Toggle from even to odd, or odd to even.
      is_even = !is_even
    end
  end

end

fruits = ['apple', 'bad apple', 'cherry', 'durian']
fruits.each_even do |fruit|
  puts "Yum!  I just love #{fruit} pies, don't you?"
end

# Remember, we are getting the even-numbered *elements*
# of the array, which in this case are all odd numbers,
# because I live only to irritate you.
[1, 2, 3, 4, 5].each_even do |odd_ball|
  puts "#{odd_ball} is NOT an even number!"
end
```

```
Yum!  I just love apple pies, don't you?
Yum!  I just love cherry pies, don't you?
1 is NOT an even number!
3 is NOT an even number!
5 is NOT an even number!
```

To pass in a block to each_even, all we had to do was stick the block after the method. You can pass a block into any method this way, though many methods will just ignore the block. In order to make your method *not* ignore the block but grab it and turn it into a proc, put the name of the proc at the end of your method's parameter list, preceded by an ampersand (&). So, that part is a little tricky but not too bad, and you have to do that only once (when you define the method). Then you can use the method over and over again, just like the built-in methods that take blocks, such as each and times. (Remember 5.times do...? What a cutie....)

If you get confused (I mean, there's this each and its block inside each_even), just remember what each_even is supposed to do: call the block passed in with every other element in the array. Once you've written it and it works, you don't need to think about what it's actually doing under the hood ("which block is called when?"); in fact, that's exactly *why* we write methods like this—so we never have to think about how they work again. We just use them.

I remember one time I wanted to *profile* some code I was writing; you know, I wanted to time how long it took to run. I wrote a method that takes the time before running the code block, then runs it, then takes the time again at the end, and finally figures out the difference. And it went a little something like this:

```ruby
def profile block_description, &block
  start_time = Time.new
  block.call
  duration = Time.new - start_time
  puts "#{block_description}:  #{duration} seconds"
end

profile '25000 doublings' do
  number = 1

  25000.times do
    number = number + number
  end

  puts "#{number.to_s.length} digits"
  #  That's the number of digits in this HUGE number.
end
profile 'count to a million' do
  number = 0
  1000000.times do
    number = number + 1
  end
end
```

```
7526 digits
25000 doublings:  0.172 seconds
count to a million:  0.218 seconds
```

How simple! How elegant! Dude, admit it: you think I'm cool. With that tiny method, we can now easily time any section of any program; we just throw the code in a block, send it to profile, and do a little dance.... What could be simpler? Though we didn't do it, you could find the slow parts of your code and add more profiling calls nested *inside* your original calls! Beautiful! In most languages, I would have to explicitly add that timing code (the stuff in profile) around every section I wanted to time. What a hassle. In Ruby, however, I get to keep it all in one place and (more important) out of my way!

14.4   A Few Things to Try

- *Even better profiling.* After you do your profiling, see the slow parts of your program, and either make them faster or learn to love them as they are, you probably don't want to see all of that profiling anymore. But (I hope) you're too lazy to go back and delete it all...especially because you might want to use it again someday. Modify the profile method so you can turn all profiling on and off by changing just one line of code. Just one word!

- *Grandfather clock.* Write a method that takes a block and calls it once for each hour that has passed today. That way, if I were to pass in the block:

```
do
    puts 'DONG!'
end
```

it would chime (sort of) like a grandfather clock. Test your method out with a few different blocks.

Hint: You can use Time.new.hour to get the current hour. However, this returns a number between 0 and 23, so you will have to alter those numbers in order to get ordinary clock-face numbers (1 to 12).

- *Program logger.* Write a method called log that takes a string description of a block (and, of course, a block). Similar to the method do_self_importantly, it should puts a string telling you it started the block and another string at the end telling you it finished and also telling you what the block returned. Test your method by sending it a code block. Inside the block, put *another* call to log, passing a block to it. In other words, your output should look something like this:

```
Beginning "outer block"...
Beginning "some little block"...
..."some little block" finished, returning:
5
Beginning "yet another block"...
..."yet another block" finished, returning:
I like Thai food!
..."outer block" finished, returning:  false
```

- *Better program logger.* The output from that last logger was kind of hard to read, and it would just get worse the more you used it. It would be so much easier to read if it indented the lines in the inner blocks. So, you'll need to keep track of how deeply nested you are every time the logger wants to write something. To do this, use a *global variable*, which is a variable you can see from anywhere in your code. To make a global variable, just precede your variable name with $, like so: $global, $nesting_depth, and $big_top_pee_wee. In the end, your logger should output code like this:

```
Beginning "outer block"...
  Beginning "some little block"...
    Beginning "teeny-tiny block"...
    ..."teeny-tiny block" finished, returning:
    lots of love
  ..."some little block" finished, returning:
  42
  Beginning "yet another block"...
  ..."yet another block" finished, returning:
  I love Indian food!
..."outer block" finished, returning:
true
```

## CHAPTER 15

Beyond This Fine Book

Well, that's about all you're going to learn from this book. Congratulations, programmer! You've learned a *lot*! Maybe you don't feel like you remember everything, or you skipped over some parts...really, that's just fine. Programming isn't about what you know; it's about what you can figure out. As long as you know where to find out the things you forgot, you're doing just fine. (I was looking stuff up constantly as I was writing this.)

Where do you look stuff up (besides here)? If there's something strange and it don't look good...who you gonna call?

I look for help with Ruby in three main places. If it's a small question, and I think I can experiment on my own to find the answer, I use irb. If it's a bigger question, I look it up in my PickAxe. And if I just can't figure it out on my own, then I ask for help on ruby-talk.

15.1 irb: Interactive Ruby

If you installed Ruby, then you installed irb. To use it, just go to your command prompt, and type *irb*. When you're in irb, you can type in any Ruby expression you want, and it will tell you the value of it. Type in *1+2*, and it will tell you 3 (note that you don't have to use puts). It's kind of like a giant Ruby calculator. When you are done, type *exit*.

There's a lot more to irb than this, but you can learn all about it in the PickAxe.

15.2 The PickAxe: *Programming Ruby*

Absolutely *the* Ruby book to get is *Programming Ruby 1.9, The Pragmatic Programmers' Guide* by Dave Thomas and others (from the Pragmatic Bookshelf).[1] Although I highly recommend picking up the third edition of this excellent book, which covers all of Ruby 1.9, you can also get an older (but still mostly relevant) version for free online.

You can find just about everything about Ruby, from the basic to the advanced, in this book. It's easy to read, it's comprehensive, and it's just about perfect. I wish every language had a book of this quality. At the back of the book, you'll find a huge section detailing every method in every class, explaining it and giving examples. (This is where you really want the third edition.) I just love this book!

You can get it from a number of places (including the Pragmatic Programmers' own site). My favorite place for the free first edition is http://ruby-doc.org/. That version has a nice table of contents on the side, as well as an index. (ruby-doc.org has lots of other great documentation as well, such as for the Core API and Standard Library...basically, it documents everything Ruby comes with right out of the box. Check it out.)

And why is it called the *PickAxe?* Well, there's a picture of a pickaxe on the cover of the book. It's a silly name, I guess, but it stuck.

15.3 Ruby-Talk: The Ruby Mailing List

Even with irb and the PickAxe, sometimes you still can't figure it out. Or perhaps you want to know whether someone already created whatever it is you are working on and want to see whether you could use it instead of writing your own. In these cases, the place to go is ruby-talk, the Ruby mailing list. It's full of friendly, smart, helpful people. People like...you know, me. To learn more about it, or to subscribe, have a look at http://www.ruby-lang.org/en/community/mailing-lists/.

WARNING: There's a *lot* of mail on the mailing list every day. I have mine automatically sent to a specific mail folder so it doesn't get in my way. If you don't want to deal with all that mail, though, you don't have to; the ruby-talk mailing list is mirrored to the newsgroup comp.lang.ruby, and vice versa, so you can see the same messages there.

15.4 Tim Toady

Something I have tried to shield you from, but that you will surely run into soon, is the concept of TMTOWTDI (pronounced *Tim Toady,* I think): There's More Than One Way To Do It.

---

1.   http://pragprog.com/book/ruby3/programming-ruby-1-9

Now some will tell you what a wonderful thing TMTOWTDI is, while others feel quite differently. I think it's pretty cool, because having more than one way to do something feels more expressive. Nonetheless, I think it's a *terrible* way to teach someone how to program. (Learning one way to do something is challenging and confusing enough.)

However, now that you are moving beyond this book, you'll be seeing much more diverse code. For example, I can think of at least five other ways to make a string (aside from surrounding some text in single quotes), and each one works slightly differently. I showed you only the simplest of the six.

And when we talked about branching, I showed you if, but I didn't show you unless. I'll let you figure that one out in irb.

Another nice little shortcut you can use with if, unless, and while is the cute one-line version:

```
#  These words are from a program I wrote to generate
#  English-like babble.  Cool, huh?
puts 'combergearl thememberate' if 5 == 2**2 + 1**1
puts 'supposine follutify' unless 'Chris'.length == 5
```

```
combergearl thememberate
```

And finally, there is another way of writing methods that take blocks (not procs). We saw the thing where we grabbed the block and turned it into a proc using the &block trick in our parameter list when we define the method. Then, to call the block, we just use block.call. Well, there's a shorter way (though I personally find it more confusing). Instead of this…

```
def do_it_twice(&block)
  block.call
  block.call
end

do_it_twice do
  puts 'murditivent flavitemphan siresent litics'
end
```

```
murditivent flavitemphan siresent litics
murditivent flavitemphan siresent litics
```

you do this…

```
def do_it_twice
  yield
  yield
end
```

```
do_it_twice do
  puts 'buritiate mustripe lablic acticise'
end
```

```
buritiate mustripe lablic acticise
buritiate mustripe lablic acticise
```

I don't know...what do you think? Maybe it's just me, but yield?! If it was something like call_the_hidden_block, that would make a *lot* more sense to me. A lot of people say yield makes sense to them. But I guess that's what TMTOWTDI is all about: they do it their way, and I'll do it my way.

15.5 THE END

You go, you big, bad programmer, you. And if you liked the book or didn't (but especially if you did), drop me a line:

chris@pine.fm

Use it for good and not for evil.

Possible Solutions

Since the first edition of this book, the single question I have been asked the most is "Where are the answers to the exercises?"

My reluctance centered around the first occurrence of the word *the* in that question.

The answers? There's more than one right answer, of course. Many, many more. These aren't math problems. Even the first exercises, which are sort of like math problems, have many possible solutions. If, instead of writing a program about orange trees or the minutes in a decade, you were asked to write a poem about them, it would be silly (if not downright harmful) to include "the answers."

That was my reasoning, anyway. Kind of stupid, in retrospect—while these aren't math problems, neither are they poems.

Still, I'm really attached to the idea that there's no one right answer here, so I did a few things to drive that point home. First, notice the title to this appendix: *possible* solutions, not *the* solutions.

Then I went through and did each exercise twice. Yes, seriously. The first time is to show just one possible way that you *could* have done it, given what you have learned up to that point in the book. The second time is to show you how I would do it, using whatever techniques tickled my fancy. Some of these techniques are not covered in this book, so it's OK if you don't understand exactly what's going on. These programs tend to be more complex but also shorter (sometimes *much* shorter) and sometimes more correct or robust. Often cuter. (I like cute code.)

No more complaining about how hard the exercises were, OK? At least you had to do them only once.

Ignore them or study them as you prefer.

A1.1 Exercises from Chapter 2

Hours in a Year

(from on page 12)

How you could do it:

```
puts 24*365
```

```
8760
```

How I would do it:

```
#  depends on if it's a leap year
puts 24*365
puts "(or #{24*366} on occasion)"
```

```
8760
(or 8784 on occasion)
```

Minutes in a Decade

(from on page 12)

How you could do it:

```
puts 60*24*(365*10 + 2)
```

```
5258880
```

How I would do it:

```
#  depends on how many leap years in that decade
puts "#{60*24*(365*10 + 2)} or #{60*24*(365*10 + 3)}"
```

```
5258880 or 5260320
```

Your Age in Seconds

(from on page 12)

How you could do it:

```
puts 60*60*24*(365*32 + 9)
```

```
1009929600
```

How I would do it:

```
puts(Time.new - Time.gm(1976, 8, 3, 13, 31))
```

```
1109222819.832
```

Our Dear Author's Age

(from on page 12)

How you could do it:

```
puts 1111000000/(60*60*24*365)
```

```
35
```

And that's pretty much how I would do it, too.

A1.2 Exercises from Chapter 5

Full Name Greeting

How you could do it:

(from on page 25)

```
puts 'What is your first name?'
f_name = gets.chomp
puts 'What is your middle name?'
m_name = gets.chomp
puts 'What is your last name?'
l_name = gets.chomp

full_name = f_name + ' ' + m_name + ' ' + l_name

puts 'Hello, ' + full_name + '!'
```

```
❮ What is your first name?
⇒ Sam
❮ What is your middle name?
⇒ I
❮ What is your last name?
⇒ Am
❮ Hello, Sam I Am!
```

How I would do it:

```
puts "What's your first name?"
f_name = gets.chomp
puts "What's your middle name?"
m_name = gets.chomp
puts "What's your last name?"
l_name = gets.chomp

puts "Chris Pine is cooler than you, #{f_name} #{m_name} #{l_name}."
```

```
❮ What's your first name?
⇒ Marvin
❮ What's your middle name?
⇒ K.
❮ What's your last name?
⇒ Mooney
❮ Chris Pine is cooler than you, Marvin K. Mooney.
```

Bigger, Better Favorite Number

How you could do it:

(from on page 25)

```
puts 'Hey!  What\'s your favorite number?'
fav_num = gets.chomp.to_i
better_num = fav_num + 1
puts 'That\'s ok, I guess, but isn\'t '+better_num.to_s+' just a bit better?'
```

❮ Hey! What's your favorite number?
⇒ **5**
❮ That's ok, I guess, but isn't 6 just a bit better?

How I would do it:

```
puts "Hey!  What's your favorite number?"
fav_num = gets.chomp.to_i
puts "That's ok, I guess, but isn't #{fav_num + 1} just a bit better?"
```

❮ Hey! What's your favorite number?
⇒ **5**
❮ That's ok, I guess, but isn't 6 just a bit better?

A1.3 Exercises from Chapter 6

Angry Boss

(from on page 32) How you could do it:

```
puts 'CAN\'T YOU SEE I\'M BUSY?!  MAKE IT FAST, JOHNSON!'
request = gets.chomp
puts 'WHADDAYA MEAN "' + request.upcase + '"?!? YOU\'RE FIRED!!'
```

❮ CAN'T YOU SEE I'M BUSY?! MAKE IT FAST, JOHNSON!
⇒ **I want a raise**
❮ WHADDAYA MEAN "I WANT A RAISE"?!? YOU'RE FIRED!!

How I would do it:

```
names = ['johnson', 'smith', 'weinberg', 'filmore']
puts "CAN'T YOU SEE I'M BUSY?!  MAKE IT FAST, #{names[rand(4)].upcase}!"
request = gets.chomp
puts "WHADDAYA MEAN \"#{request.upcase}\"?!? YOU'RE FIRED!!"
```

❮ CAN'T YOU SEE I'M BUSY?! MAKE IT FAST, FILMORE!
⇒ **I quit**
❮ WHADDAYA MEAN "I QUIT"?!? YOU'RE FIRED!!

Table of Contents

(from on page 32) How you could do it:

```
title  = 'Table of Contents'.center(50)
chap_1 = 'Chapter 1:  Getting Started'.ljust(30) + 'page  1'.rjust(20)
chap_2 = 'Chapter 2:  Numbers'.ljust(30)        + 'page  9'.rjust(20)
chap_3 = 'Chapter 3:  Letters'.ljust(30)        + 'page 13'.rjust(20)
```

```
puts title
puts
puts chap_1
puts chap_2
puts chap_3
```

```
            Table of Contents

Chapter 1:  Getting Started         page  1
Chapter 2:  Numbers                 page  9
Chapter 3:  Letters                 page 13
```

And how would I do it? Well, that was a different exercise (at the end of Chapter 8).

A1.4 Exercises from Chapter 7

"99 Bottles of Beer on the Wall"

How you could do it:

(from on page 49)

```
num_at_start = 5   #  change to 99 if you want

num_now = num_at_start

while num_now > 2
  puts num_now.to_s + ' bottles of beer on the wall, ' +
       num_now.to_s + ' bottles of beer!'
  num_now = num_now - 1

  puts 'Take one down, pass it around, ' +
       num_now.to_s + ' bottles of beer on the wall!'
end

puts "2 bottles of beer on the wall, 2 bottles of beer!"
puts "Take one down, pass it around, 1 bottle of beer on the wall!"
puts "1 bottle of beer on the wall, 1 bottle of beer!"
puts "Take one down, pass it around, no more bottles of beer on the wall!"
```

```
5 bottles of beer on the wall, 5 bottles of beer!
Take one down, pass it around, 4 bottles of beer on the wall!
4 bottles of beer on the wall, 4 bottles of beer!
Take one down, pass it around, 3 bottles of beer on the wall!
3 bottles of beer on the wall, 3 bottles of beer!
Take one down, pass it around, 2 bottles of beer on the wall!
2 bottles of beer on the wall, 2 bottles of beer!
Take one down, pass it around, 1 bottle of beer on the wall!
1 bottle of beer on the wall, 1 bottle of beer!
Take one down, pass it around, no more bottles of beer on the wall!
```

How I would do it:

```
num_at_start = 5  #  change to 99 if you want

num_bot = proc { |n| "#{n} bottle#{n == 1 ? '' : 's'}" }

num_at_start.downto(2) do |num|
  puts "#{num_bot[num]} of beer on the wall, #{num_bot[num]} of beer!"
  puts "Take one down, pass it around, #{num_bot[num-1]} of beer on the wall!"
end

puts "#{num_bot[1]} of beer on the wall, #{num_bot[1]} of beer!"
puts "Take one down, pass it around, no more bottles of beer on the wall!"
```

```
5 bottles of beer on the wall, 5 bottles of beer!
Take one down, pass it around, 4 bottles of beer on the wall!
4 bottles of beer on the wall, 4 bottles of beer!
Take one down, pass it around, 3 bottles of beer on the wall!
3 bottles of beer on the wall, 3 bottles of beer!
Take one down, pass it around, 2 bottles of beer on the wall!
2 bottles of beer on the wall, 2 bottles of beer!
Take one down, pass it around, 1 bottle of beer on the wall!
1 bottle of beer on the wall, 1 bottle of beer!
Take one down, pass it around, no more bottles of beer on the wall!
```

Deaf Grandma

(from on page 49) How you could do it:

```
puts 'HEY THERE, SONNY!  GIVE GRANDMA A KISS!'

while true
  said = gets.chomp

  if said == "BYE"
    puts 'BYE SWEETIE!'
    break
  end

  if said != said.upcase
    puts 'HUH?!  SPEAK UP, SONNY!'
  else
    random_year = 1930 + rand(21)
    puts 'NO, NOT SINCE ' + random_year.to_s + '!'
  end
end
```

```
< HEY THERE, SONNY!  GIVE GRANDMA A KISS!
⇒ hi, grandma
< HUH?!  SPEAK UP, SONNY!
⇒ HI, GRANDMA!
< NO, NOT SINCE 1945!
⇒ HOW YOU DOING?
< NO, NOT SINCE 1933!
⇒ I SAID, HOW YOU DOING?
< NO, NOT SINCE 1944!
⇒ OK
```

```
‹ NO, NOT SINCE 1934!
⇒ BYE
‹ BYE SWEETIE!
```

How I would do it:

```
puts 'HEY THERE, SONNY!  GIVE GRANDMA A KISS!'

while true
  said = gets.chomp

  break if said == "BYE"
  response = if said != said.upcase
    'HUH?!  SPEAK UP, SONNY!'
  else
    "NO, NOT SINCE #{1930 + rand(21)}!"
  end

  puts response
end

puts 'BYE SWEETIE!'
```

```
‹ HEY THERE, SONNY!  GIVE GRANDMA A KISS!
⇒ hi, grandma
‹ HUH?!  SPEAK UP, SONNY!
⇒ HI, GRANDMA!
‹ NO, NOT SINCE 1950!
⇒ HOW YOU DOING?
‹ NO, NOT SINCE 1936!
⇒ I SAID, HOW YOU DOING?
‹ NO, NOT SINCE 1947!
⇒ OK
‹ NO, NOT SINCE 1949!
⇒ BYE
‹ BYE SWEETIE!
```

Deaf Grandma Extended

How you could do it:

(from on page 49)

```
puts 'HEY THERE, PEACHES!  GIVE GRANDMA A KISS!'
bye_count = 0
while true
  said = gets.chomp
  if said == 'BYE'
    bye_count = bye_count + 1
  else
    bye_count = 0
  end
  if bye_count >= 3
    puts 'BYE-BYE CUPCAKE!'
    break
  end
end
```

```ruby
  if said != said.upcase
    puts 'HUH?!  SPEAK UP, SONNY!'
  else
    random_year = 1930 + rand(21)
    puts 'NO, NOT SINCE ' + random_year.to_s + '!'
  end
end
```

❬ HEY THERE, PEACHES! GIVE GRANDMA A KISS!
⇒ **HI, GRANDMA!**
❬ NO, NOT SINCE 1940!
⇒ **BYE**
❬ NO, NOT SINCE 1938!
⇒ **BYE**
❬ NO, NOT SINCE 1944!
⇒ **ADIOS, MUCHACHA!**
❬ NO, NOT SINCE 1947!
⇒ **BYE**
❬ NO, NOT SINCE 1934!
⇒ **BYE**
❬ NO, NOT SINCE 1933!
⇒ **BYE**
❬ BYE-BYE CUPCAKE!

How I would do it:

```ruby
puts 'HEY THERE, PEACHES!  GIVE GRANDMA A KISS!'
bye_count = 0

while true
  said = gets.chomp
  if said == 'BYE'
    bye_count += 1
  else
    bye_count  = 0
  end
  break if bye_count >= 3

  response = if said != said.upcase
    'HUH?!  SPEAK UP, SONNY!'
  else
    "NO, NOT SINCE #{1930 + rand(21)}!"
  end

  puts response
end

puts 'BYE-BYE CUPCAKE!'
```

❬ HEY THERE, PEACHES! GIVE GRANDMA A KISS!
⇒ **HI, GRANDMA!**
❬ NO, NOT SINCE 1935!
⇒ **BYE**

```
‹ NO, NOT SINCE 1930!
⇒ BYE
‹ NO, NOT SINCE 1931!
⇒ ADIOS, MUCHACHA!
‹ NO, NOT SINCE 1937!
⇒ BYE
‹ NO, NOT SINCE 1937!
⇒ BYE
‹ NO, NOT SINCE 1936!
⇒ BYE
‹ BYE-BYE CUPCAKE!
```

Leap Years

How you could do it:

(from on page 49)

```ruby
puts 'Pick a starting year (like 1973 or something):'
starting = gets.chomp.to_i

puts 'Now pick an ending year:'
ending   = gets.chomp.to_i

puts 'Check it out... these years are leap years:'
year = starting

while year <= ending
  if year%4 == 0
    if year%100 != 0 || year%400 == 0
      puts year
    end
  end

  year = year + 1
end
```

```
‹ Pick a starting year (like 1973 or something):
⇒ 1973
‹ Now pick an ending year:
⇒ 1977
‹ Check it out... these years are leap years:
  1976
```

How I would do it:

```ruby
puts 'Pick a starting year (like 1973 or something):'
starting = gets.chomp.to_i
puts 'Now pick an ending year:'
ending   = gets.chomp.to_i
puts 'Check it out... these years are leap years:'
(starting..ending).each do |year|
  next if year%4   != 0
  next if year%100 == 0 && year%400 != 0
  puts year
end
```

```
‹ Pick a starting year (like 1973 or something):
⇒ 1973
‹ Now pick an ending year:
⇒ 1977
‹ Check it out... these years are leap years:
1976
```

A1.5 Exercises from Chapter 8

Building and Sorting an Array

(from on page 56) How you could do it:

```ruby
puts 'Give me some words, and I will sort them:'
words = []

while true
  word = gets.chomp
  if word == ''
    break
  end

  words.push word
end

puts 'Sweet!  Here they are, sorted:'
puts words.sort
```

```
‹ Give me some words, and I will sort them:
⇒ banana
⇒ apple
⇒ cherry
⇒
‹ Sweet!  Here they are, sorted:
apple
banana
cherry
```

How I would do it:

```ruby
puts 'Give me some words, and I will sort them:'
words = []

while true
  word = gets.chomp
  break if word.empty?

  words << word
end

puts 'Sweet!  Here they are, sorted:'
puts words.sort
```

```
❮ Give me some words, and I will sort them:
⇒ banana
⇒ apple
⇒ cherry
⇒
❮ Sweet!  Here they are, sorted:
  apple
  banana
  cherry
```

Table of Contents, Revisited

How you could do it:

(from on page 56)

```
title    = 'Table of Contents'

chapters = [['Getting Started',  1],
            ['Numbers',          9],
            ['Letters',         13]]

puts title.center(50)
puts

chap_num = 1

chapters.each do |chap|
  name = chap[0]
  page = chap[1]

  beginning = 'Chapter ' + chap_num.to_s + ':  ' + name
  ending    = 'page ' + page.to_s

  puts beginning.ljust(30) + ending.rjust(20)
  chap_num = chap_num + 1
end
```

```
                    Table of Contents

Chapter 1:  Getting Started            page 1
Chapter 2:  Numbers                    page 9
Chapter 3:  Letters                    page 13
```

How I would do it:

```
title    = 'Table of Contents'

chapters = [['Getting Started',  1],
            ['Numbers',          9],
            ['Letters',         13]]

puts title.center(50)
puts
chapters.each_with_index do |chap, idx|
  name, page = chap
  chap_num   = idx + 1
```

```
    beginning = "Chapter #{chap_num}:  #{name}"
    ending    = "page #{page}"

    puts beginning.ljust(30) + ending.rjust(20)
end
```

```
                    Table of Contents

Chapter 1:  Getting Started                  page 1
Chapter 2:  Numbers                          page 9
Chapter 3:  Letters                          page 13
```

A1.6 Exercises from Chapter 9

Improved ask Method

(from on page 68) How you could do it:

```
def ask question
  while true
    puts question
    reply = gets.chomp.downcase
    if reply == 'yes'
      return true
    end
    if reply -- 'no'
      return false
    end
    #  If we got this far, then we're going to loop
    #  and ask the question again.
    puts 'Please answer "yes" or "no".'
  end
end
likes_it = ask 'Do you like eating tacos?'
puts likes_it
```

```
‹ Do you like eating tacos?
⇒ yes
‹ true
```

How I would do it:

```
def ask question
  while true
    puts question
    reply = gets.chomp.downcase
    return true  if reply == 'yes'
    return false if reply == 'no'
    puts 'Please answer "yes" or "no".'
  end
end
puts(ask('Do you like eating tacos?'))
```

```
‹ Do you like eating tacos?
⇒ yes
‹ true
```

Old-School Roman Numerals

How you could do it:

(from on page 68)

```
def old_roman_numeral num
  roman = ''

  roman = roman + 'M' * (num            / 1000)
  roman = roman + 'D' * (num % 1000 /  500)
  roman = roman + 'C' * (num %  500 /  100)
  roman = roman + 'L' * (num %  100 /   50)
  roman = roman + 'X' * (num %   50 /   10)
  roman = roman + 'V' * (num %   10 /    5)
  roman = roman + 'I' * (num %    5 /    1)
  roman
end
puts(old_roman_numeral(1999))
```

```
MDCCCCLXXXXVIIII
```

How I would do it:

```
def old_roman_numeral num
  raise 'Must use positive integer' if num <= 0
  roman = ''

  roman << 'M' * (num            / 1000)
  roman << 'D' * (num % 1000 /  500)
  roman << 'C' * (num %  500 /  100)
  roman << 'L' * (num %  100 /   50)
  roman << 'X' * (num %   50 /   10)
  roman << 'V' * (num %   10 /    5)
  roman << 'I' * (num %    5 /    1)

  roman
end
puts(old_roman_numeral(1999))
```

```
MDCCCCLXXXXVIIII
```

"Modern" Roman Numerals

How you could do it:

(from on page 68)

```
def roman_numeral num
  thous = (num            / 1000)
  hunds = (num % 1000 /  100)
  tens  = (num %  100 /   10)
  ones  = (num %   10        )

  roman = 'M' * thous
```

```
  if hunds == 9
    roman = roman + 'CM'
  elsif hunds == 4
    roman = roman + 'CD'
  else
    roman = roman + 'D' * (num % 1000 / 500)
    roman = roman + 'C' * (num %  500 / 100)
  end

  if tens == 9
    roman = roman + 'XC'
  elsif tens == 4
    roman = roman + 'XL'
  else
    roman = roman + 'L' * (num %  100 /  50)
    roman = roman + 'X' * (num %   50 /  10)
  end

  if ones == 9
    roman = roman + 'IX'
  elsif ones == 4
    roman = roman + 'IV'
  else
    roman = roman + 'V' * (num %   10 /   5)
    roman = roman + 'I' * (num %    5 /   1)
  end

  roman
end

puts(roman_numeral(1999))
```

```
MCMXCIX
```

How I would do it:

```
def roman_numeral num
  raise 'Must use positive integer' if num <= 0

  digit_vals = [['I',    5,    1],
                ['V',   10,    5],
                ['X',   50,   10],
                ['L',  100,   50],
                ['C',  500,  100],
                ['D', 1000,  500],
                ['M',  nil, 1000]]

  roman = ''
  remaining = nil

  # Build string "roman" in reverse.
  build_rev = proc do |l,m,n|
    num_l = m ? (num % m / n) : (num / n)
    full  = m && (num_l == (m/n - 1))
```

```
    if full && (num_l>1 || remaining)
      # must carry
      remaining ||= l # carry l if not already carrying
    else
      if remaining
        roman << l + remaining
        remaining = nil
      end

      roman << l * num_l
    end
  end

  digit_vals.each {|l,m,n| build_rev[l,m,n]}

  roman.reverse
end

puts(roman_numeral(1999))
```

MIM

A1.7 Exercises from Chapter 10

Rite of Passage: Sorting

How you could do it:

(from on page 74)

```
def sort arr
  rec_sort arr, []
end

def rec_sort unsorted, sorted
  if unsorted.length <= 0
    return sorted
  end

  # So if we got here, then it means we still
  #  have work to do.
  smallest      = unsorted.pop
  still_unsorted = []

  unsorted.each do |tested_object|
    if tested_object < smallest
      still_unsorted.push smallest
      smallest = tested_object
    else
      still_unsorted.push tested_object
    end
  end

  # Now "smallest" really does point to the
  #  smallest element that "unsorted" contained,
  #  and all the rest of it is in "still_unsorted".
```

```
  sorted.push smallest

  rec_sort still_unsorted, sorted
end

puts(sort(['can','feel','singing','like','a','can']))
```

```
a
can
can
feel
like
singing
```

How I would do it (well, aside from just using the built-in sort method):

```
#  The well-known quicksort algorithm.
def sort arr
  return arr if arr.length <= 1

  middle = arr.pop
  less   = arr.select{|x| x <  middle}
  more   = arr.select{|x| x >= middle}

  sort(less) + [middle] + sort(more)
end

p(sort(['can','feel','singing','like','a','can']))
```

```
["a", "can", "can", "feel", "like", "singing"]
```

Shuffle

(from on page 75) How you could do it:

```
def shuffle arr
  shuf = []
  while arr.length > 0
    # Randomly pick one element of the array.
    rand_index = rand(arr.length)

    # Now go through each item in the array,
    # putting them all into new_arr except for the
    # randomly chosen one, which goes into shuf.
    curr_index = 0
    new_arr = []

    arr.each do |item|
      if curr_index == rand_index
        shuf.push item
      else
        new_arr.push item
      end

      curr_index = curr_index + 1
    end
```

```
    # Replace the original array with the new,
    # smaller array.
    arr = new_arr
  end

  shuf
end
```

```
puts(shuffle([1,2,3,4,5,6,7,8,9]))
```

```
9
8
6
1
3
5
2
7
4
```

How I would do it:

```
def shuffle arr
  arr.sort_by{rand}
end
```

```
p(shuffle([1,2,3,4,5,6,7,8,9]))
```

```
[9, 5, 3, 2, 6, 4, 8, 7, 1]
```

Dictionary Sort

How you could do it:

(from on page 75)

```
def dictionary_sort arr
  rec_dict_sort arr, []
end
def rec_dict_sort unsorted, sorted
  if unsorted.length <= 0
    return sorted
  end
  # So if we got here, then it means we still
  # have work to do.
  smallest      = unsorted.pop
  still_unsorted = []

  unsorted.each do |tested_object|
    if tested_object.downcase < smallest.downcase
      still_unsorted.push smallest
      smallest = tested_object
    else
      still_unsorted.push tested_object
    end
  end
```

```
  #  Now "smallest" really does point to the
  #  smallest element that "unsorted" contained,
  #  and all the rest of it is in "still_unsorted".
  sorted.push smallest

  rec_dict_sort still_unsorted, sorted
end

puts(dictionary_sort(['can','feel','singing.','like','A','can']))
```

```
A
can
can
feel
like
singing.
```

How I would do it:

```
#  The well-known quicksort algorithm.
def dictionary_sort arr
  return arr if arr.length <= 1

  middle = arr.pop
  less   = arr.select{|x| x.downcase <  middle.downcase}
  more   = arr.select{|x| x.downcase >= middle.downcase}

  dictionary_sort(less) + [middle] + dictionary_sort(more)
end

words = ['can','feel','singing.','like','A','can']
puts(dictionary_sort(words).join(' '))
```

```
A can can feel like singing.
```

Expanded english_number

(from on page 81) How you could do it:

```
def english_number number
  if number < 0  # No negative numbers.
    return 'Please enter a number that isn\'t negative.'
  end
  if number == 0
    return 'zero'
  end

  # No more special cases!  No more returns!
  num_string = ''  # This is the string we will return.
  ones_place = ['one',      'two',      'three',
                'four',     'five',     'six',
                'seven',    'eight',    'nine']
  tens_place = ['ten',      'twenty',   'thirty',
                'forty',    'fifty',    'sixty',
                'seventy',  'eighty',   'ninety']
```

```
teenagers  = ['eleven',    'twelve',    'thirteen',
              'fourteen',  'fifteen',   'sixteen',
              'seventeen', 'eighteen',  'nineteen']

zillions = [['hundred',             2],
            ['thousand',            3],
            ['million',             6],
            ['billion',             9],
            ['trillion',           12],
            ['quadrillion',        15],
            ['quintillion',        18],
            ['sextillion',         21],
            ['septillion',         24],
            ['octillion',          27],
            ['nonillion',          30],
            ['decillion',          33],
            ['undecillion',        36],
            ['duodecillion',       39],
            ['tredecillion',       42],
            ['quattuordecillion',  45],
            ['quindecillion',      48],
            ['sexdecillion',       51],
            ['septendecillion',    54],
            ['octodecillion',      57],
            ['novemdecillion',     60],
            ['vigintillion',       63],
            ['googol',            100]]

#  "left" is how much of the number
#         we still have left to write out.
#  "write" is the part we are
#         writing out right now.
#  write and left...get it?  :)
left  = number

while zillions.length > 0
  zil_pair = zillions.pop
  zil_name =        zil_pair[0]
  zil_base = 10 ** zil_pair[1]
  write = left/zil_base          # How many zillions left?
  left  = left - write*zil_base  # Subtract off those zillions.

  if write > 0
    # Now here's the recursion:
    prefix = english_number write
    num_string = num_string + prefix + ' ' + zil_name

    if left > 0
      # So we don't write 'two billionfifty-one'...
      num_string = num_string + ' '
    end
  end
end
end
```

```ruby
  write = left/10          # How many tens left?
  left  = left - write*10  # Subtract off those tens.

  if write > 0
    if ((write == 1) and (left > 0))
      # Since we can't write "tenty-two" instead of
      # "twelve", we have to make a special exception
      #  for these.
      num_string = num_string + teenagers[left-1]
      # The "-1" is because teenagers[3] is
      #  'fourteen', not 'thirteen'.

      # Since we took care of the digit in the
      # ones place already, we have nothing left to write.
      left = 0
    else
      num_string = num_string + tens_place[write-1]
      # The "-1" is because tens_place[3] is
      #  'forty', not 'thirty'.
    end

    if left > 0
      # So we don't write 'sixtyfour'...
      num_string = num_string + '-'
    end
  end

  write = left  # How many ones left to write out?
  left  = 0     # Subtract off those ones.

  if write > 0
    num_string = num_string + ones_place[write-1]
    # The "-1" is because ones_place[3] is
    #  'four', not 'three'.
  end

  # Now we just return "num_string"...
  num_string
end

puts english_number(  0)
puts english_number(  9)
puts english_number( 10)
puts english_number( 11)
puts english_number( 17)
puts english_number( 32)
puts english_number( 88)
puts english_number( 99)
puts english_number(100)
puts english_number(101)
puts english_number(234)
puts english_number(3211)
puts english_number(999999)
```

```
puts english_number(1000000000000)
puts english_number(1092387451029385601298347092853602384759823745610 34)
```

```
zero
nine
```

```
ten
eleven
seventeen
thirty-two
eighty-eight
ninety-nine
one hundred
one hundred one
two hundred thirty-four
three thousand two hundred eleven
nine hundred ninety-nine thousand nine hundred ninety-nine
one trillion
one hundred nine quindecillion two hundred
   thirty-eight quattuordecillion seven hundred forty-five ...
```

And that's just about how I would do it, too.

Wedding Number

I *told* you I didn't do this one. It was a joke! Move on! (from on page 81)

"Ninety-nine Bottles of Beer on the Wall."

How you could do it: (from on page 81)

```
# english_number as above, plus this:
num_at_start = 5  #  change to 9999 if you want
num_now = num_at_start
while num_now > 2
  puts english_number(num_now).capitalize + ' bottles of beer on the wall, ' +
      english_number(num_now) + ' bottles of beer!'
  num_now = num_now - 1
  puts 'Take one down, pass it around, ' +
      english_number(num_now) + ' bottles of beer on the wall!'
end

puts "Two bottles of beer on the wall, two bottles of beer!"
puts "Take one down, pass it around, one bottle of beer on the wall!"
puts "One bottle of beer on the wall, one bottle of beer!"
puts "Take one down, pass it around, no more bottles of beer on the wall!"
```

```
Five bottles of beer on the wall, five bottles of beer!
Take one down, pass it around, four bottles of beer on the wall!
Four bottles of beer on the wall, four bottles of beer!
Take one down, pass it around, three bottles of beer on the wall!
Three bottles of beer on the wall, three bottles of beer!
Take one down, pass it around, two bottles of beer on the wall!
```

```
Two bottles of beer on the wall, two bottles of beer!
Take one down, pass it around, one bottle of beer on the wall!
One bottle of beer on the wall, one bottle of beer!
Take one down, pass it around, no more bottles of beer on the wall!
```

How I would do it:

```
# english_number as above, plus this:

num_at_start = 5  #  change to 9999 if you want

num_bot = proc { |n| "#{english_number n} bottle#{n == 1 ? '' : 's'}" }

num_at_start.downto(2) do |num|
  bottles =
  puts "#{num_bot[num]} of beer on the wall, #{num_bot[num]} of beer!".capitalize
  puts "Take one down, pass it around, #{num_bot[num-1]} of beer on the wall!"
end
puts "#{num_bot[1]} of beer on the wall, #{num_bot[1]} of beer!".capitalize
puts "Take one down, pass it around, no more bottles of beer on the wall!"
```

```
Five bottles of beer on the wall, five bottles of beer!
Take one down, pass it around, four bottles of beer on the wall!
Four bottles of beer on the wall, four bottles of beer!
Take one down, pass it around, three bottles of beer on the wall!
Three bottles of beer on the wall, three bottles of beer!
Take one down, pass it around, two bottles of beer on the wall!
Two bottles of beer on the wall, two bottles of beer!
Take one down, pass it around, one bottle of beer on the wall!
One bottle of beer on the wall, one bottle of beer!
Take one down, pass it around, no more bottles of beer on the wall!
```

A1.8 Exercises from Chapter 11

Safer Picture Downloading

(from on page 92) Well, since I was asking you to adapt it to *your* computer, I can't really show you how to do it. I will show you the program I *actually* wrote, though.

It's a bit more complex that the other examples here, partly because it's a real, working tool.

```
#  For Katy, with love.

###  Download pictures from camera card.

require 'win32ole'

STDOUT.sync = true
Thread.abort_on_exception = true

Dir.chdir 'C:\Documents and Settings\Chris\Desktop\pictureinbox'

#  Always look here for pics.
```

```ruby
pic_names = Dir['!undated/**/*.{jpg,avi}']
thm_names = Dir['!undated/**/*.{thm}'     ]

# Scan for memory cards in the card reader.
WIN32OLE.new("Scripting.FileSystemObject").Drives.each() do |x|
  #driveType 1 is removable disk
  if x.DriveType == 1 && x.IsReady
    pic_names += Dir[x.DriveLetter+':/**/*.{jpg,avi}']
    thm_names += Dir[x.DriveLetter+':/**/*.{thm}'     ]
  end
end

months = %w(jan feb mar apr may jun jul aug sep oct nov dec)

encountered_error = false

print "Downloading #{pic_names.size} files:  "

pic_names.each do |name|
  print '.'
  is_movie = (name[-3..-1].downcase == 'avi')

  if is_movie
    orientation = 0
    new_name = File.open(name) do |f|
      f.seek(0x144,IO::SEEK_SET)
      f.read(20)
    end

    new_name[0...3] = '%.2d' % (1 + months.index(new_name[0...3].downcase))
    new_name = new_name[-4..-1] + ' ' + new_name[0...-5]
  else
    new_name, orientation = File.open(name) do |f|
      f.seek(0x36, IO::SEEK_SET)
      orientation_ = f.read(1)[0]
      f.seek(0xbc, IO::SEEK_SET)
      new_name_ = f.read(19)
      [new_name_, orientation_]
    end
  end

  [4,7,10,13,16].each {|n| new_name[n] = '.'}
  if new_name[0] != '2'[0]
    encountered_error = true
    puts "\n"+'ERROR:  Could not process "'+name+
      '" because it\'s not in the proper format!'
    next
  end

  save_name = new_name + (is_movie ? '.orig.avi' : '.jpg')
  # Make sure we don't save over another file!!
  while FileTest.exist? save_name
    new_name += 'a'
    save_name = new_name + (is_movie ? '.orig.avi' : '.jpg')
  end
```

```
    case orientation
      when 6
        `convert "#{name}" -rotate "90>"  "#{save_name}"`
        File.delete name
      when 8
        `convert "#{name}" -rotate "-90>" "#{save_name}"`
        File.delete name
      else
        File.rename name, save_name
    end
end
print "\nDeleting #{thm_names.size} THM files:   "
thm_names.each do |name|
  print '.'
  File.delete name
end
# If something bad happened, make sure she
# sees the error message before the window closes.
if encountered_error
  puts
  puts "Press [Enter] to finish."
  puts
  gets
end
```

Build Your Own Playlist

(from on page 92) How you could do it:

```
# using the shuffle method as defined above
all_oggs = shuffle(Dir['**/*.ogg'])

File.open 'playlist.m3u', 'w' do |f|
  all_oggs.each do |ogg|
    f.write ogg+"\n"
  end
end
puts 'Done!'
```

And that's exactly how I'd do it, too.

Build a Better Playlist

(from on page 93) How you could do it:

```
def music_shuffle filenames
  # We don't want a perfectly random shuffle, so let's
  # instead do a shuffle like card-shuffling.  Let's
  # shuffle the "deck" twice, then cut it once.  That's
  # not enough times to make a perfect shuffle, but it
  # does mix things up a bit.
```

```ruby
  # Before we do anything, let's actually *sort* the
  # input, since we don't know how shuffled it might
  # already be, and we don't want it to be *too* random.
  filenames = filenames.sort
  len       = filenames.length

  # Now we shuffle twice.
  2.times do
    l_idx = 0     # index of next card in left pile
    r_idx = len/2 # index of next card in right pile
    shuf  = []
    # NOTE:  If we have an odd number of "cards",
    #        then the right pile will be larger.

    while shuf.length < len
      if shuf.length%2 == 0
        # take card from right pile
        shuf.push(filenames[r_idx])
        r_idx = r_idx + 1
      else
        # take card from left pile
        shuf.push(filenames[l_idx])
        l_idx = l_idx + 1
      end
    end

    filenames = shuf
  end
  # And cut the deck.
  arr = []
  cut = rand(len) # index of card to cut at
  idx = 0

  while idx < len
    arr.push(filenames[(idx+cut)%len])
    idx = idx + 1
  end

  arr
end
songs = ['aa/bbb',  'aa/ccc',   'aa/ddd',
         'AAA/xxxx', 'AAA/yyyy', 'AAA/zzzz', 'foo/bar']
puts(music_shuffle(songs))
```

```
aa/bbb
aa/ddd
AAA/xxxx
AAA/zzzz
aa/ccc
foo/bar
AAA/yyyy
```

Well, that's OK, I guess. It's not all that random, and maybe if you had a larger playlist you'd want to shuffle it three or four times...I don't really know.

A better way would be mix more carefully and on every level (genre, artist, album). For example, if I have a playlist that is two-thirds lounge and one-third jazz, I want a jazz song roughly every third song (and rarely two in a row and *never* three in a row). Further, if I had, among all the jazz songs, only two by Kurt Elling (travesty, I know), then one should be *somewhere* in the first half of the playlist, and the other should be *somewhere* in the last half. (But where in the respective halves they appear should be truly random.) And all these constraints must be met simultaneously.

What I do is find similar songs (let's say songs on the same CD), mix them up, and spread them out as far away from each other as I can in the next grouping (say, songs by the same artist). Then I do the same for the next level up (say, genre). The nice thing is that this algorithm is recursive, so I can add levels for free if I want. For example, I have a Billie Holiday CD with multiple recordings of one of the songs. I like it, but I'd like those to be spread out as far from each other as possible in the playlist (while respecting all other constraints at higher levels). No problem—I just make a directory inside the CD directory and move the similar recordings all in there, and the recursion takes care of the rest!

Enough talk; here's how I would do it:

```ruby
def music_shuffle filenames
  songs_and_paths = filenames.map do |s|
    [s, s.split('/')]  # [song, path]
  end

  tree = {:root => []}

  # put each song into the tree
  insert_into_tree = proc do |branch, song, path|
    if path.length == 0 # add to current branch
      branch[:root] << song
    else # delve deeper
      sub_branch = path[0]
      path.shift # like "pop", but pops off the front

      if !branch[sub_branch]
        branch[sub_branch] = {:root => []}
      end

      insert_into_tree[branch[sub_branch], song, path]
    end
  end

  songs_and_paths.each{|sp| insert_into_tree[tree, *sp]}
```

```
#  recursively:
#    - shuffle sub-branches (and root)
#    - weight each sub-branch (and root)
#    - merge (shuffle) these groups together
shuffle_branch = proc do |branch|
  shuffled_subs = []

  branch.each do |key, unshuffled|
    shuffled_subs << if key == :root
      unshuffled # At this level, these are all duplicates.
    else
      shuffle_branch[unshuffled]
    end
  end

  weighted_songs = []

  shuffled_subs.each do |shuffled_songs|
    shuffled_songs.each_with_index do |song, idx|
      num = shuffled_songs.length.to_f
      weight = (idx + rand) / num
      weighted_songs << [song, weight]
    end
  end

  weighted_songs.sort_by{|s,v| v}.map{|s,v| s}
  end

  shuffle_branch[tree]
end

songs = ['aa/bbb',  'aa/ccc',  'aa/ddd',
        'AAA/xxxx', 'AAA/yyyy', 'AAA/zzzz', 'foo/bar']

puts(music_shuffle(songs))
```

```
foo/bar
aa/ccc
AAA/yyyy
AAA/zzzz
aa/bbb
aa/ddd
AAA/xxxx
```

It might be hard to tell with such a tiny playlist, but with 500 songs you really begin to appreciate how well this method works.

A1.9 Exercises from Chapter 12

One Billion Seconds!

Well, I don't know your brithday, so I don't know how you'd do it, but here's how I would do it: (from on page 97)

```
#  I don't know what second I was born.
puts(Time.gm(1976, 8, 3, 13, 31) + 10**9)

#  And yes, I had a party.  It was awesome
#  (at least the parts I remember).
```

Fri Apr 11 15:17:40 UTC 2008

Happy Birthday!

(from on page 97)

How you could do it:

```
puts 'What year were you born?'
b_year = gets.chomp.to_i

puts 'What month were you born?  (1-12)'
b_month = gets.chomp.to_i

puts 'What day of the month were you born?'
b_day = gets.chomp.to_i

b = Time.local(b_year, b_month, b_day)
t = Time.new

age = 1

while Time.local(b_year + age, b_month, b_day) <= t
  puts 'SPANK!'
  age = age + 1
end
```

```
< What year were you born?
⇒ 2002
< What month were you born?  (1-12)
⇒ 2
< What day of the month were you born?
⇒ 20th
< SPANK!
  SPANK!
  SPANK!
  SPANK!
  SPANK!
  SPANK!
  SPANK!
  SPANK!
  SPANK!
```

How I would do it:

```
puts 'Hey, when were you born?  (Please use YYYYMMDD format.)'
input = gets.chomp

b_year  = input[0..3].to_i
b_month = input[4..5].to_i
b_day   = input[6..7].to_i
```

```
t = Time.new

t_year  = t.year
t_month = t.month
t_day   = t.day

age = t_year - b_year

if t_month < b_month || (t_month == b_month && t_day < b_day)
  age -= 1
end

if t_month == b_month && t_day == b_day
  puts 'HAPPY BIRTHDAY!!'
end

age.times { puts 'SPANK!' }
```

```
‹ Hey, when were you born?  (Please use YYYYMMDD format.)
⇒ 20020220
‹ SPANK!
  SPANK!
  SPANK!
  SPANK!
  SPANK!
  SPANK!
  SPANK!
  SPANK!
  SPANK!
```

Party Like It's roman_to_integer mcmxcix!

How you could do it:

(from on page 101)

```ruby
def roman_to_integer roman
  digit_vals = {'i' =>    1,
                'v' =>    5,
                'x' =>   10,
                'l' =>   50,
                'c' =>  100,
                'd' =>  500,
                'm' => 1000}
  total = 0
  prev  = 0
  index = roman.length - 1
  while index >= 0
    c = roman[index].downcase
    index = index - 1
    val = digit_vals[c]
    if !val
      puts 'This is not a valid roman numeral!'
      return
    end
```

```
    if val < prev
      val = val * -1
    else
      prev = val
    end
    total = total + val
  end

  total
end

puts(roman_to_integer('mcmxcix'))
puts(roman_to_integer('CCCLXV'))
```

```
1999
365
```

How I would do it:

```
def roman_to_integer roman
  digit_vals = {'i' =>     1,
                'v' =>     5,
                'x' =>    10,
                'l' =>    50,
                'c' =>   100,
                'd' =>   500,
                'm' =>  1000}
  total = 0
  prev  = 0
  roman.reverse.each_char do |c_or_C|
    c   = c_or_C.downcase
    val = digit_vals[c]
    if !val
      puts 'This is not a valid roman numeral!'
      return
    end
    if val < prev
      val *= -1
    else
      prev = val
    end
    total += val
  end

  total
end

puts(roman_to_integer('mcmxcix'))
puts(roman_to_integer('CCCLXV'))
```

```
1999
365
```

Birthday Helper!

How you could do it:

(from on page 101)

```ruby
#  First, load in the birthdates.
birth_dates = {}
File.read('birthdates.txt').each_line do |line|
  line = line.chomp
  #  Find the index of first comma,
  #  so we know where the name ends.
  first_comma = 0
  while line[first_comma] != ',' &&
        first_comma < line.length
    first_comma = first_comma + 1
  end

  name = line[0..(first_comma - 1)]
  date = line[-12..-1]

  birth_dates[name] = date
end

#  Now ask the user which one they want to know.
puts 'Whose birthday would you like to know?'
name = gets.chomp
date = birth_dates[name]

if date == nil
  puts "Oooh, I don't know that one..."
else
  puts date[0..5]
end
```

‹ Whose birthday would you like to know?
⇒ **Christopher Plummer**
‹ Dec 13

How I would do it:

```ruby
#  First, load in the birthdates.
birth_dates = {}

File.readlines('birthdates.txt').each do |line|
  name, date, year = line.split(',')
  birth_dates[name] = Time.gm(year, *(date.split))
end

#  Now ask the user which one they want to know.
puts 'Whose birthday would you like to know?'
name = gets.chomp
bday = birth_dates[name]

if bday == nil
  puts "Oooh, I don't know that one..."
else
```

```
  now = Time.new
  age = now.year - bday.year

  if now.month > bday.month || (now.month == bday.month && now.day > bday.day)
    age += 1
  end

  if now.month == bday.month && now.day == bday.day
    puts "#{name} turns #{age} TODAY!!"
  else
    date = bday.strftime "%b %d"
    puts "#{name} will be #{age} on #{date}."
  end
end
```

```
‹ Whose birthday would you like to know?
⇒ Christopher Pine
‹ Christopher Pine will be 36 on Aug 03.
```

A1.10 Exercises from Chapter 13

Extend the Built-in Classes

(from on page 104) How you could do it:

```
class Array
  def shuffle
    arr = self
    #  Now we can just copy the old shuffle method.
    shuf = []

    while arr.length > 0
      # Randomly pick one element of the array.
      rand_index = rand(arr.length)

      # Now go through each item in the array,
      # putting them all into new_arr except for
      # the randomly chosen one, which goes into
      # shuf.
      curr_index = 0
      new_arr = []
      arr.each do |item|
        if curr_index == rand_index
          shuf.push item
        else
          new_arr.push item
        end

        curr_index = curr_index + 1
      end

      # Replace the original array with the new,
      # smaller array.
```

```ruby
      arr = new_arr
    end
    shuf
  end
end
class Integer
  def factorial
    if self <= 1
      1
    else
      self * (self-1).factorial
    end
  end
  def to_roman
    #  I chose old-school roman numerals just to save space.
    roman = ''

    roman = roman + 'M' * (self        / 1000)
    roman = roman + 'D' * (self % 1000 /  500)
    roman = roman + 'C' * (self %  500 /  100)
    roman = roman + 'L' * (self %  100 /   50)
    roman = roman + 'X' * (self %   50 /   10)
    roman = roman + 'V' * (self %   10 /    5)
    roman = roman + 'I' * (self %    5 /    1)

    roman
  end
end

puts [1,2,3,4,5].shuffle
puts  7.factorial
puts 73.to_roman
```

```
3
5
4
1
2
5040
LXXIII
```

How I would do it:

```ruby
class Array
  def shuffle
    sort_by{rand}  #  "self" is implied, remember?
  end
end
class Integer
  def factorial
    raise 'Must not use negative integer' if self < 0
    (self <= 1) ? 1 : self * (self-1).factorial
  end
```

```ruby
  def to_roman
    # I chose old-school roman numerals just to save space.
    raise 'Must use positive integer' if self <= 0

    roman = ''

    roman << 'M' * (self        / 1000)
    roman << 'D' * (self % 1000 /  500)
    roman << 'C' * (self %  500 /  100)
    roman << 'L' * (self %  100 /   50)
    roman << 'X' * (self %   50 /   10)
    roman << 'V' * (self %   10 /    5)
    roman << 'I' * (self %    5 /    1)

    roman
  end
end

# Get ready for the pure awesome...
p 7.factorial.to_roman.split(//).shuffle
```

```
["X", "X", "M", "M", "M", "X", "M", "X", "M"]
```

Orange Tree

(from on page 112)

How you could do it:

```ruby
class OrangeTree
  def initialize
    @height       = 0
    @orange_count = 0
    @alive        = true
  end

  def height
    if @alive
      @height
    else
      'A dead tree is not very tall.  :('
    end
  end

  def count_the_oranges
    if @alive
      @orange_count
    else
      'A dead tree has no oranges.  :('
    end
  end

  def one_year_passes
    if @alive
      @height = @height + 0.4
      @orange_count = 0 # old oranges fall off
```

```
    if @height > 10 && rand(2) > 0
      # tree dies
      @alive = false
      'Oh, no!  The tree is too old, and has died.  :('
    elsif @height > 2
      # new oranges grow
      @orange_count = (@height * 15 - 25).to_i
      "This year your tree grew to #{@height}m tall," +
      " and produced #{@orange_count} oranges."
    else
      "This year your tree grew to #{@height}m tall," +
      " but is still too young to bear fruit."
    end
  else
    'A year later, the tree is still dead.  :('
  end
end
def pick_an_orange
  if @alive
    if @orange_count > 0
      @orange_count = @orange_count - 1
      'You pick a juicy, delicious orange!'
    else
      'You search every branch, but find no oranges.'
    end
  else
    'A dead tree has nothing to pick.  :('
  end
end
end
ot = OrangeTree.new
23.times do
  ot.one_year_passes
end
puts(ot.one_year_passes)
puts(ot.count_the_oranges)
puts(ot.height)
puts(ot.one_year_passes)
puts(ot.one_year_passes)
puts(ot.one_year_passes)
puts(ot.one_year_passes)
puts(ot.one_year_passes)
puts(ot.height)
puts(ot.count_the_oranges)
puts(ot.pick_an_orange)
```

```
This year your tree grew to 9.6m tall, and produced 119 oranges.
119
9.6
This year your tree grew to 10.0m tall, and produced 125 oranges.
Oh, no! The tree is too old, and has died. :(
```

```
A year later, the tree is still dead. :(
A year later, the tree is still dead. :(
A year later, the tree is still dead. :(
A dead tree is not very tall. :(
A dead tree has no oranges. :(
A dead tree has nothing to pick. :(
```

That's pretty much how I would do it, too: clean and simple.

Interactive Baby Dragon

(from on page 112)

How you could do it:

```ruby
#  using the Dragon class from the chapter
puts 'What would you like to name your baby dragon?'
name = gets.chomp
pet  = Dragon.new name

while true
  puts
  puts 'commands:  feed, toss, walk, rock, put to bed, exit'
  command = gets.chomp

  if command == 'exit'
    exit
  elsif command == 'feed'
    pet.feed
  elsif command == 'toss'
    pet.toss
  elsif command == 'walk'
    pet.walk
  elsif command == 'rock'
    pet.rock
  elsif command == 'put to bed'
    pet.put_to_bed
  else
    puts 'Huh?  Please type one of the commands.'
  end
end
```

How I would do it:

```ruby
#  using the Dragon class from the chapter
puts 'What would you like to name your baby dragon?'
name = gets.chomp
pet  = Dragon.new name
obj  = Object.new # just a blank, dummy object

while true
  puts
  puts 'commands:  feed, toss, walk, rock, put_to_bed, exit'

  command = gets.chomp
```

```ruby
  if command == 'exit'
    exit
  elsif pet.respond_to?(command) && !obj.respond_to?(command)
    #  I only want to accept methods that dragons have,
    #  but that regular objects *don't* have.
    pet.send command
  else
    puts 'Huh?  Please type one of the commands.'
  end
end
```

A1.11 Exercises from Chapter 14

Even Better Profiling

How you could do it:

(from on page 120)

```ruby
def profile block_description, &block
  #  To turn profiling on/off, set this
  #  to true/false.

  profiling_on = false

  if profiling_on
    start_time = Time.new
    block.call

    duration = Time.new - start_time
    puts "#{block_description}:  #{duration} seconds"
  else
    block.call
  end
end
```

How I would do it:

```ruby
$OPT_PROFILING_ON = false

def profile block_description, &block
  if $OPT_PROFILING_ON
    start_time = Time.new
    block[]
    duration = Time.new - start_time
    puts "#{block_description}:  #{duration} seconds"
  else
    block[]
  end
end
```

Grandfather Clock

(from on page 120) How you could do it:

```ruby
def grandfather_clock &block
  hour = Time.new.hour

  if hour >= 13
    hour = hour - 12
  end

  if hour == 0
    hour = 12
  end

  hour.times do
    block.call
  end
end
grandfather_clock do
  puts 'DONG!'
end
```

```
DONG!
DONG!
```

How I would do it:

```ruby
def grandfather_clock &block
  hour = (Time.new.hour + 11)%12 + 1

  hour.times(&block)
end

grandfather_clock { puts 'DONG!' }
```

```
DONG!
DONG!
```

Program Logger

(from on page 120) How you could do it:

```ruby
def log desc, &block
  puts 'Beginning "' + desc + '"...'
  result = block.call
  puts '..."' + desc + '" finished, returning:  ' + result.to_s
end
log 'outer block' do
  log 'some little block' do
    1**1 + 2**2
  end

  log 'yet another block' do
    '!doof iahT ekil I'.reverse
```

```
    end

  '0' == 0
end
```

```
Beginning "outer block"...
Beginning "some little block"...
..."some little block" finished, returning:  5
Beginning "yet another block"...
..."yet another block" finished, returning:  I like Thai food!
..."outer block" finished, returning:  false
```

How I would do it:

```
def log desc, &block
  puts "Beginning #{desc.inspect}..."
  result = block[]
  puts "...#{desc.inspect} finished, returning:  #{result}"
end

log 'outer block' do
  log 'some little block' do
    1**1 + 2**2
  end

  log 'yet another block' do
    '!doof iahT ekil I'.reverse
  end

  '0' == 0
end
```

```
Beginning "outer block"...
Beginning "some little block"...
..."some little block" finished, returning:  5
Beginning "yet another block"...
..."yet another block" finished, returning:  I like Thai food!
..."outer block" finished, returning:  false
```

Better Program Logger

How you could do it:

(from on page 120)

```
$logger_depth = 0

def log desc, &block
  prefix = '  '*$logger_depth
  puts prefix + 'Beginning "' + desc + '"...'

  $logger_depth = $logger_depth + 1
  result = block.call
  $logger_depth = $logger_depth - 1

  puts prefix + '..."' + desc + '" finished, returning:  ' + result.to_s
end
```

```
log 'outer block' do
  log 'some little block' do
    log 'teeny-tiny block' do
      'lOtS oF lOVe'.downcase
    end

    7 * 3 * 2
  end

  log 'yet another block' do
    '!doof naidnI evol I'.reverse
  end

  '0' == "0"
end
```

```
Beginning "outer block"...
  Beginning "some little block"...
    Beginning "teeny-tiny block"...
    ..."teeny-tiny block" finished, returning:  lots of love
  ..."some little block" finished, returning:  42
  Beginning "yet another block"...
  ..."yet another block" finished, returning:  I love Indian food!
..."outer block" finished, returning:  true
```

How I would do it:

```
$logger_depth = 0

def log desc, &block
  prefix = '  '*$logger_depth
  puts prefix+"Beginning #{desc.inspect}..."
  $logger_depth += 1
  result = block[]
  $logger_depth -= 1
  puts prefix+"...#{desc.inspect} finished, returning:  #{result}"
end

log 'outer block' do
  log 'some little block' do
    log 'teeny-tiny block' do
      'lOtS oF lOVe'.downcase
    end
    7 * 3 * 2
  end

  log 'yet another block' do
    '!doof naidnI evol I'.reverse
  end
  '0' == "0"
end
```

```
Beginning "outer block"...
  Beginning "some little block"...
    Beginning "teeny-tiny block"...
    ..."teeny-tiny block" finished, returning:  lots of love
  ..."some little block" finished, returning:  42
  Beginning "yet another block"...
  ..."yet another block" finished, returning:  I love Indian food!
..."outer block" finished, returning:  true
```

Index

Just Starting Out?

Here's the help you need to find and navigate the new job.

It's your first day on the new job. You've got the programming chops, you're up on the latest tech, you're sitting at your workstation... now what? *New Programmer's Survival Manual* gives your career the jolt it needs to get going: essential industry skills to help you apply your raw programming talent and make a name for yourself. It's a no-holds-barred look at what *really* goes on in the office—and how to not only survive, but thrive in your first job and beyond.

Josh Carter
(250 pages) ISBN: 9781934356814. $29
http://pragmaticprogrammer.com/titles/jcdeg

You've got the technical chops — the skills to get a great job doing what you love. Now it's time to get down to the business of planning your job search, focusing your time and attention on the job leads that matter, and interviewing to wow your boss-to-be. Land the tech job you love.

Coding Tony: "The book gives very good tips on how to write a good résumé, and how to avoid clichés...I recommend the book, even if you aren't looking for a job... for now.." See the full review

Andy Lester
(280 pages) ISBN: 9781934356265. $23.95
http://pragmaticprogrammer.com/titles/algh

The New Web

See how to manage the latest CSS, HTML, and all the rest of the plumbing you need for the modern web.

HTML5 and CSS3 are the future of web development, but you don't have to wait to start using them. Even though the specification is still in development, many modern browsers and mobile devices already support HTML5 and CSS3. This book gets you up to speed on the new HTML5 elements and CSS3 features you can use right now, and backwards compatible solutions ensure that you don't leave users of older browsers behind.

Brian P. Hogan
(280 pages) ISBN: 9781934356685. $33
http://pragmaticprogrammer.com/titles/bhh5

Modern web development takes more than just HTML and CSS with a little JavaScript mixed in. Clients want more responsive sites with faster interfaces that work on multiple devices, and you need the latest tools and techniques to make that happen. This book gives you more than 40 concise, tried-and-true solutions to to-day's web development problems, and introduces new workflows that will expand your skillset.

Brian P. Hogan, Chris Warren, Mike Weber, Chris Johnson, Aaron Godin
(325 pages) ISBN: 9781934356838. $35
http://pragmaticprogrammer.com/titles/wbdev

Be Agile

Don't just "do" agile; you want *be* agile. We'll show you how.

The best agile book isn't a book: *Agile in a Flash* is a unique deck of index cards that fit neatly in your pocket. You can tape them to the wall. Spread them out on your project table. Get stains on them over lunch. These cards are meant to be used, not just read.

Jeff Langr and Tim Ottinger
(110 pages) ISBN: 9781934356715. $15
http://pragmaticprogrammer.com/titles/olag

Here are three simple truths about software development:

1. You can't gather all the requirements up front. 2. The requirements you do gather will change. 3. There is always more to do than time and money will allow.

Those are the facts of life. But you can deal with those facts (and more) by becoming a fierce software-delivery professional, capable of dispatching the most dire of software projects and the toughest delivery schedules with ease and grace.

Jonathan Rasmusson
(280 pages) ISBN: 9781934356586. $34.95
http://pragmaticprogrammer.com/titles/jtrap